JUSTICE, PEACE,
and the Future of the
POLICE

JUSTICE, PEACE,
and the Future of the
POLICE

How to Dig Deep and Do What's
Right—from the Inside

Monica Hunter-Alexander

LIONCREST
PUBLISHING

Justice, Peace, and the Future of the Police

How to Dig Deep and Do What's Right—from the Inside

ISBN 978-1-5445-3153-3 Hardcover
      978-1-5445-3152-6 Paperback
      978-1-5445-3151-9 Ebook

To Johnny, the love of my life. You have encouraged me,
stood by me, and supported my dreams, goals, and aspirations.

To Spencer, my teammate and the best son I could
have EVER asked for. You sacrificed a lot when you were young,
but you always seemed proud to be my son. I am blessed and honored
to have both you and Johnny in my cheering section.

To Felicia, my best friend in the whole wide world.
I know I would not have made it this far without your love,
honesty, and encouragement.

To Lauren, my niece. You have believed in me your entire life.
We are connected souls tied together by love, commitment, and drive.
Thank you for asking me, "Auntie Ca, when are you
going to write your book?" Until I did it!

To Megan, thank you for your support, energy, love,
and dedication to me and this process.

To Kamala, my dear friend. Thank you for making me a
part of your family more than forty years ago when
we met at North Texas State University.

To Vernestine, my mentor. You are no longer with us
on this earth. However, you are truly the epitome of not enjoying
the shade of the trees you planted. I hope you can see how much
your guidance, encouragement, and support meant—
and still mean—to me.

Contents

Introduction

The Sankofa Bird has been adopted as a symbol of what Africana Studies strives to do. The word *"Sankofa"* can be translated to mean, *"go back to the past and bring forward that which is useful."* The bird is rendered as twisting its beak behind itself, in order to bring forth an egg from its back.

Connecting the past with the present allows us to be more effective agents in shaping our understanding of the forces that will have an impact on our collective future as citizens of the planet. We all share the responsibility for defining the terms by which we live. We honor those who have shown us the way and taught us the strategies for survival, endurance and growth.[1]

—Southern Illinois University-Carbondale School of Africana and Multicultural Studies

---

[1] https://cola.siu.edu/africanastudies/about-us/sankofa.php#:~:text=The%20word%20%22Sankofa%22%20can%20be,an%20egg%20from%20its%20back.

I am an African American woman, a twenty-three-year veteran of the Washington State Patrol (WSP), and the executive director of the Washington State Criminal Justice Training Commission (WSCJTC).

I probably look very good on paper. However, I still find myself fighting to be seen as a dynamic, competent, and dedicated leader in the world of law enforcement. The irony is that for the same reasons I look good on paper, I am discounted in real life.

I am used to navigating among multiple roles and different kinds of treatment, and I apply that perspective to the work I do today in training the future of law enforcement in Washington State.

I often ask myself, why don't people want to talk about race? Especially those who work in policing? Is it because it is an uncomfortable conversation? Because it is scary? Are people afraid they will say something unintentionally that will offend someone? How do we move forward? If we don't talk about race, it becomes further embedded in a system we refuse to see. How do we begin these difficult conversations? Let's talk about that as we go on this journey in this book together.

I can see the Black Lives Matter (BLM) versus Blue Lives Matter discussion from multiple angles because I know how hard the separation of community and law enforcement has been on under-served communities. I also know that when law enforcement loses a sister or brother in blue, the pain is real. Not all cops are bad, and not all cops are racist. Many start in the force at a very young age with little life experience. The lack of life experience contributes to the fear of the conversation about race and equity.

There is a great reason to recruit young people for the law enforce-ment profession. Police officers work long hours, rotating shifts, miss a lot of holidays with family, and give up a large part of their youth to protect and serve. A challenge with recruiting young people is that they bring limited life experience and even less emotional maturity. Even though our role is to protect and serve, so many police are fine with being aggressive and confrontational, going off on citizens and demanding their ID over the smallest infraction.

When the police kill a man, in daylight hours, on a crowded street, knowing they are being videotaped, with other officers look-ing on (or not, because they turned their backs while Mr. Floyd was dying and begging for his life), Houston we have a prob-lem. Many might say, "We don't know what happened before the video started!" or "We weren't there!" We cannot justify all police encounters. There are times we have to stand for justice and say, "That was wrong. Period." That is how law enforcement regains credibility with the community we serve. Like George Floyd, however, people want to make excuses or justify excessive force. There's a bully mentality that must be corrected. We cannot continue to police this way in America and expect to maintain a civil society.

The police uniform is confrontational all by itself. When I'm wearing a gun, I don't need to add more aggression on top of that presentation. So many people who benefit from the system and the power it wields over our society don't even realize it's broken or why. Others do realize it and don't want to confront it.

That's part of the reason I'm writing this book.

To help confront that system.

To inspire positive change.

To give new perspective to decision makers in law enforcement and the people who make decisions with and for law enforcement.

To lift up all who will come after me in this field.

To share my experiences with my son, Spencer, who is now a police officer.

PASSING THE TORCH

Spencer has been telling me since he was four years old that we'd patrol together one day. I wish that would have happened. Although during my final week before I retired, he went on a ride-along with me. That was a great day!

I worry for Spencer. Yes, for his safety, but also because I want him to always make the right choices. I want him to lead and be strong enough that if he sees someone holding another man like George Floyd down, he will say, "Let him up."

There's no defense for suffocating someone. At the same time, we need to have an open conversation about the holes in policing. We don't know what Derek Chauvin was thinking when he responded to the call of a fake twenty-dollar bill. And of course, even if Floyd knowingly used a forged bill, that's not a crime punishable by death.

I tell my son never to lose what I taught him. I've shown him how we treat people no matter what. We only use force in order to save our own lives or the lives of others. And we communicate with dignity and respect.

I learned this lesson long ago when I was a flight attendant. In that job, all you have are your words. You do not have a gun belt with multiple tools on your hip. When I became a police officer, it was like the communication-first attitude went out the window—and I caught onto that quickly. When I was on my two-month coaching trip after the WSP academy, my coach and I responded to a hit-and-run collision of a WSP trooper on his motorcycle. The driver was arrested, but no one could get him to talk. They put the suspect in the backseat of our car. My coach said I should be the one to talk to him because "I knew how to communicate with people." Everyone was so impressed by how the man opened up to me.

Do you want to know my secret?

I said, "Hi, my name is Monica. What's your name?"

I treated him like a person. That's it. And unfortunately, especially in cases of escalation, that does not always happen.

I have dedicated this phase of my career to making it the rule.

WHAT TO EXPECT IN THIS BOOK

As you can probably already tell from reading only this far, I shoot straight—figuratively and literally. (Though I did need a little extra help when I entered the academy with zero experience with a gun, a story I'll share with you later.) You can expect more of that as you read—more of the truth as I've experienced it, yes, but also more of the lessons I've learned from those experiences.

Those lessons, and the stories of how I learned them, make up the chapters. We'll cover the following, and then some:

- What it means to trust yourself, and how important that is in this profession

- The value of mentorship and nurturing meaningful relationships

- What it truly means to face obstacles and overcome them

- What it means to own both your successes and your failures

- The value of listening first, not fighting first

- The value of hard work, discipline, and sacrifice

- The importance of building bridges

- The power of tenacity and doing what's right for the community

- What diversity means to the future of policing

- What's in store for law enforcement as new training protocols are implemented

- And much more

I know I'm not a perfect person, a perfect trooper, or a perfect leader. Those things are impossible. But I know that I'm honest, I've got something important to say, and I've always done what I felt was right (even when it was unpopular). What I feel is right today is sharing my story with you so that we can make things better.

Let's get started.

1

The End and the Beginning, in That Order

"Spencer, would you like to introduce our guest today?"

I stood in front of my son's kindergarten class, in full uniform, ready to speak. It was September 1998, and I'd graduated from the academy in May of that year. His teacher had asked if I could talk to the class about being a policewoman and bring my patrol car for the kids to look at.

I said yes, of course. At the time, I'd thought it was just going to be my son's class, but the teacher had invited all the kindergarteners. It was a packed room full of wiggly kids, chatter, and energy—and I was at the front of it. Spencer came up and stood beside me.

At that moment, I thought back to what we'd just gone through together: my being at the academy, living there Monday through Friday for six months. It had felt more like six years, being away from Spencer. Every Sunday night, he would say, "Mommy, don't go!"

"Mommy has to go and earn her trooper hat," I'd tell him.

"Okay, Mommy!"

It was our routine, and he was very strong during this time.

But after about five months, he broke down. I remember it vividly: my friend Linda, whom I carpooled with, came to pick me up at six one Sunday evening. When Spencer saw me get my suitcase, he grabbed my leg and screamed.

"PLEASE DON'T GO!"

I said what I always did.

"Mommy has to get her trooper hat."

But this time, his response broke my heart.

"I don't care about that hat. Please don't go!" he wailed, hurling himself into a full-blown fit. I tried to work my way toward the door, Spencer still attached to my leg. Mercifully, Linda said she'd be back early the next morning to pick me up.

"Stay with Spencer," she whispered. I was so thankful. I certainly knew how hard being away from Spencer was for me, but at that moment, I knew how hard it was for him. He'd been managing the schedule so well up to that point, but that experience taught me that everyone has their breaking point.

That night, I snuggled my son and slowed everything down for both of us. I explained the importance of completing what you start. I told him I only had one month left. I told him Mommy could not quit now.

The next morning, when Linda arrived, it was my turn to cry. But I told myself exactly what I'd told Spencer the night before: that I had to complete what I started. For both of us.

Seven months later, there I was, standing in front of his classroom. Him by my side, waiting to be introduced.

What would he say? Would he say something about the hat we'd talked about for all that time? Or about the cool sirens on the car?

He didn't say any of that. Instead, he peered up at me, grinning.

"That's my mom."

Tears fell down my cheeks in that moment because it felt like so much came into view for him right then: the fact that his mother was a state trooper now, that all the hard work and long days and nights in the academy when he didn't want me to leave had led up to something. To this.

Many people told me that as Spencer got older, he'd outgrow his "that's my mom" pride. But it hasn't happened yet, and I'm so grateful.

* * *

I don't see many people who look like me in this profession. I don't see many women, and I definitely don't see many African American women.

Being an African American woman doesn't automatically make me a good police officer. Being Monica made me a good police officer, partly because I know how important it is for officers to identify with the communities they serve. My presence helps the police department overcome some of its barriers and hurdles. At the same time, I'm a voice for people because I think a little differently and draw on my life experiences to solve problems and overcome obstacles.

I did not have a bad relationship with the police growing up. In fact, I worked in a donut shop. Yes, I really did work in a donut shop and later got into law enforcement. It was destined to happen (by the way, I LOVE donuts). During my time there, a number of Pasadena police officers came in regularly for their morning coffee. I worked every Saturday and Sunday morning. It was a nice area, and they were always kind to me. They'd see me walking home from work and say hi on their PA. For some reason, their acknowledging me made me feel special. I felt protected by their actions.

As I got older, I heard more stories about how the police treated African American people and all the events in Los Angeles involving police, gangs, and violence, and I began to see how my little donut world was not really reflective of the big world outside of my somewhat safe existence. It came to a head for me when I saw the video of Rodney King. This was jarring and scary. It was one of the earliest instances of seeing such violence on a home video camera. I thought, *What is happening?*

I don't remember exactly when I first saw footage of the beating, but I know I watched it over and over. King flailed around on the ground as police beat him. I felt fear that the police could behave with such violence, that an officer would repeatedly strike a person with a baton while also tasing him. Then there was the picture of King afterward, which was shocking. I recall not knowing what to think as I tried to process my feelings about this terrible time…one that would soon become a historical event. How would this event divide our communities? I was sure there would be violence. I knew this was the beginning of something terrible.

During the trial of the police officers that beat King prior to arresting him, people gathered on the courthouse steps every day, waiting for news. Would the officers be found guilty? Would they walk free and go back to their jobs to beat another person? What would the community's reaction be? When the verdict was announced, the riots ensued. During that time, I became hyper-conscious of how bad the relationship was between the police and the community.

LA was on fire. People were breaking windows and looting. I watched in absolute disbelief.

I'll never forget one scene I saw unfold on television: a few protesters pulled Reginald Denny, a white man, out of his cement mixer truck. He was just driving down the street and probably didn't even know the verdict had been announced. Denny may not have even been in tune to what was happening with King and the police. Three African American men opened Denny's door, pulled him onto the ground, and began beating him. I watched as the men hit him repeatedly. They finished the beating off by hitting Denny in the head with a brick. I thought he was dead.

Another African American man, Titus Murphy, saw the situation unfolding on *his* TV, and he recognized the location. He left his house and bravely put himself in harm's way, trying to reach Denny. The visual of Murphy dragging Denny's body back into the cement truck—while the man was bloodied and probably dying—is etched in my mind. He then proceeded to drive him to safety through escalating chaos in the streets—the definition of heroic. He saved his life.

At that moment, I saw African American men angry at years of violence at the hands of the police. They made the wrong choice and put their hands on a white man, very nearly killing him. That same white man was ultimately saved by another African American man who made the *right* choice. It's a circle of pain, of sadness, of courage, and of heart. And I will never forget it.

Later, I saw Denny on the Phil Donahue show, and he was forgiving of what happened. Murphy came on the show, too. When asked why he put his life on the line, he said, "It was just the right thing to do." He'd go on to say that he believed in one race: the human race.

I've never ever gotten over what I saw that day. Titus Murphy was more inspiring that day than anyone I'd ever seen. He knew he had to help, even at risk to himself, which included facing off against protesters with guns.

If not for him, a man would have bled to death in the street and died. To this day, it boggles my mind how much good and how much evil can be present all in the same space.

I do understand the rage and the sadness of the protesters, in a way. I've felt rage myself listening to misinformed and uninformed people speak about issues of race. At the same time, as an African American person, I know that when another African American person does something wrong, we all feel it. In a way, society makes us all pay. People treat us with fear as a collective, and we have to shoulder the sadness and the burden for each other, whether we want to or not.

This incident triggered something within me that changed the course of my life forever. I wanted to pursue a calling that would allow me to do the right thing, like Titus. I wanted to be a part of the solution.

Before that day, even though I knew a lot of cops, I didn't want to be a police officer. Growing up I wanted to be a makeup artist, a clothing designer, or a hairdresser. Becoming a cop didn't fit my wardrobe. I didn't want anybody to tell me what to wear every day. (Even though, as a flight attendant, I was told what to wear and how to wear my hair. I was even told what size earrings I could wear, and we could not display toe cleavage. I had never heard of toe cleavage before I was hired by United Airlines.)

When I owned my hair salon, I could do whatever I wanted and wear my hair however I wanted. I loved that freedom.

But Titus Murphy ignited something inside of me that I could not ignore.

I wanted to participate in a greater change, which was clearly necessary. Now that I've been on this journey for twenty-five years, I feel the same. And it is still clearly more necessary than ever.

THE ONLY ONE

Before my current role, I was a twenty-three-year state trooper. When I joined the state patrol, I knew there were no commissioned African American females in the WSP, meaning officers who carry a gun and have law enforcement powers. If I hadn't known that fact, I would have learned quickly, because people reminded me every step of my hiring process, my background check, and my psychological interview. They constantly told me there were no other African American female state troopers. They were uncomfortable with my race and gender. I was thirty-four years old, and I knew I was an African American woman.

As I began my journey looking for a law enforcement organization to join, I selected the WSP because it was a great organization, based on what I needed. It had the best benefits and the best working conditions. At that time in my life, benefits mattered. I knew I was about to be a single mother to Spencer. I was going to have to figure out how to live my calling and take care of my son.

And so, as I'll unpack in these chapters, for twenty-three years I worked my way through the ranks. I tested for sergeant early and endured ridicule for wanting to move ahead in my career. I did it anyway, because I believed it was the right thing to do for the agency, my community, Spencer, and MY career.

Most officers thought I wouldn't make the cut the first time I took the test. Their doubt told me I was on the right track. I thought that if they cared so much about the test—and if they thought it was so hard that there was no way I could have placed so highly—then there must have been something really great on the other side. It made me study harder…including while my son spent hours at the skating rink, which was what he loved to do. I took my books with me everywhere. I lost sleep, waking up at four in the morning to study before going to work. It was the beginning and end of each day. Though there were study groups formed, I was never invited to be part of them. I didn't let it get to me, and I didn't waste time. I read. I studied the agency from a global perspective, which most troopers did not do. At the time, I was a spokesperson for the agency, so I knew how to craft a sentence easily in front of people and under pressure.

All along, I felt convinced I could get my detractors on board, help them see who I was, and bring them to understand I cared about what was good for the organization and the community. If I succeeded, I'd be happy. Even if I was not liked for trying. I didn't get into law enforcement to make new best friends, though I certainly made some along my way. In fact, one of my favorite memories of my early career is when I was scheduled to work on Christmas Day, and one of my colleagues said, "You're not working that day. You need to be with your kid." He took my shift, voluntarily missing the holiday with his own family because he knew I was a single mom. I cherish those positive memories that pepper my career—of *good* cops being *good* people and doing *good* things.

Unfortunately, there are plenty of stories to tell that are the opposite of that Christmas Day, but the people who didn't like me could not stop my journey. I was there to serve the people, which will always be my purpose, even after I leave law enforcement.

Of course, I still felt the anger coming toward me and knew how people talked about me. I wasn't immune, but it also didn't stop me. Every once in a while, I'd confront the person running their mouth the most and ask if I could speak with them for a minute. Then, I'd repeat their words back to them and make them really uncomfortable. It is one thing to say negative things about a person if you don't have to say it to them directly. But when you find yourself facing the person you said such negative words about, the game changes. That is when I would feel empowered. I'd tell them I was always interested in learning how to be a better person, so if they had comments about how I should do my job, they should just come and talk to me. They might try to deny it, and I'd say we didn't have to argue—I just wanted them to handle issues differently moving forward. I'd say we should work together, and then I'd "thank them" and move on, feeling like I just made an interception and was moving toward a touchdown!

I wouldn't act in anger, but they'd feel the fire in my words anyway because I'd address the behavior head-on. I've always been here to serve, so I use my strength to cut through the BS and keep the focus on communities. I've learned if you have the courage to confront people directly, you can stop rumors, lies, and exaggeration before it gets the gas to go too far. If you let the gossip and the misrepresentations fester, they get bigger and bigger, taking on a life of their own.

Ultimately, I placed first on the sergeant exam out of approximately 210 people. I was promoted to the rank of sergeant on August 15, 2003. At that time, I was the first and only African American female to have been promoted in the history of the WSP.

Yes, you read that right. The first one.

As of this writing (in 2021), the WSP still has only one African American female sergeant. Because I was the first to place number one on the list, that created doubt and disbelief. People had no idea how important this opportunity was for me. I wish the agency understood how important having that diversity in the ranks was to the growth and development of the WSP and the law enforcement profession. It did not have to be me, but it was—and I was beyond excited and happy to be in the game at the next level.

Having employed that tactic of facing challenges head-on throughout my career, maybe it's fitting that my last confrontation was with the chief.

FORCED INTO RETIREMENT

I have many stories to share with you in this book, and one of the most pivotal happened at the end of my career with the WSP. Let's start at the end so you have context for what's to come:

It was near the end of my twenty-two-year career (I just didn't know it yet) when I found myself sitting in the chief's office.

I'd been working as the legislative liaison for four years at that point—the most difficult assignment for a captain in the WSP. And I hadn't phoned it in…I'd moved the needle. I'd helped to secure $11 million for a high-throughput lab to process over 10,000 backlogged sexual assault kits that had been sitting on shelves in police stations across the state of Washington. I helped secure raises for troopers, lieutenants, and captains. I'd done groundbreaking work to call attention to missing and murdered Indigenous women in the state, holding meeting after meeting in an effort to get something done.

One morning, the chief called me into his office and said he needed to know whether I wanted to continue to be the legislative liaison or was I ready for change. He said he knew it was a grind job, that I'd done well, and that he'd understand if I wanted to move on. He built me up and said I could think about it—I didn't have to let him know right then.

A week later, I went back and said I *did* want to change. I told him I'd love the opportunity to do something else. I hadn't taken off more than a week at a time for over four years. I never took sick leave. You simply can't miss a piece of legislation or an opportunity to speak on a bill without negative consequences. If you fail to give input, it could jeopardize your agency. I'd always performed my role with conscientiousness and responsibility.

I was ready to try something else and recharge, to some degree, and I told him as much. He said he'd get back to me.

I was on a break just down the street from headquarters when I received a call from the chief's executive assistant saying the chief wanted to see me as soon as possible. I felt excited, assuming he'd be generous with me and reward my loyalty and hard work. I was ready to receive something good. I canceled my tea order and rushed back to meet him. He was finishing up a phone call, and then he summoned me in.

The chief told me he'd decided to put me in the Human Resources Division (HRD). Now, a couple of years earlier, I'd told my husband if I got assigned to HRD, I'd start looking to retire because I couldn't go from one grind to another. At that point, I'd only been the legislative liaison for two years, and I already knew I was going to burn out. I thought I'd stayed long enough to have earned the privilege of being like the other captains, going on a new adventure—even just being able to take real vacations and lunch breaks would have been nice.

Here I'd worked on and fought for some massive bills, and I thought the chief appreciated my work. I figured he'd tell me the positions opening up and give me some choices. I was the senior captain of those being moved, and rank matters. Plus, I was so close to retirement.

But none of that happened.

"I'm sorry?" I said, shocked.

He repeated his decision—which would have *decreased* my pay and impacted my retirement funds. (I was two years out from retirement, and our pension is based on our highest two years—but my reassignment represented a pay cut. So not only was he sending me to another grind, but he was also taking away part of my pay. He said it was only 5 percent over half a year, but it all matters when we're adding up our retirement. He knew the impact, and he demoted me.)

After the grind I'd been on for four years, HRD represented one of the worst assignments I could get—plus I'd be financially demoted. Yes, I was still a captain, but I was convinced the chief knew what he was doing. If he did not, I reminded him of the impact his decision would have on me. I was exhausted, and HRD needed a lot of work. The number of women and people of color in the entire agency was unfortunately low and didn't reflect the demographics of our communities. Some of the employees were disgruntled and frustrated. I did not in any way want the assignment, but the culture is such that when the chief gives you something, you just say, "Yes, sir—thank you, sir," even if it's raw liver. You swallow it. I couldn't, though. I had to say my piece, even if it made him stop liking me. He told me he'd been sent on HRD for six months once upon a time and it was one of the best things ever to happen for him.

I repeated my objection, and he asked me what I wanted. I said I wanted to go to a district. I thought it was important for me to work in a district, because you never want to lose touch with what's happening on the street and to troopers. At every rank, I would make it a point to go out and work the road. Periodically, in fact, I'd go out and stop cars because I wanted to remember how people treated troopers. I wanted to always remember the tough job our field force did. I also liked contacting and educating people.

After most people reach a certain level, they could take or leave a district, but I wanted to stay in the mix. If I couldn't have that kind of position, then I would have taken something like internal affairs. I had experience in internal affairs. I wanted to make a real impact. I also felt like a pawn, because there wasn't much diversity in HRD, so it seemed like sending the African American woman there to check a box.

When I mentioned the district option, he told me he couldn't move someone else, even though he did so all the time. He gave me no choice and even put a captain who was junior to me in the open internal affairs role, which I would have gladly taken. I could not help but feel he was trying to make things more difficult for me.

I found out later through the grapevine the chief *was* punishing me, as I'd suspected. I don't know exactly what I did, but it upset him enough that he told a couple of people, "Let's see how she does down there." At the time, I wondered if he'd done it on purpose, and then later, I got confirmation.

He didn't listen to my argument, so I said, "Thank you" and walked out the door. A few members of my staff were in a conference room outside his office, working on a project. Most of the big conference rooms are glass, so they saw me get called into the chief's office and then walk out. They were worried because they knew I was going to be reassigned but not where. They were hoping they could go with me. However, they could tell that when I walked out of that meeting, something bad had happened.

I don't remember anything after the meeting other than driving home. It was early in the afternoon. I obviously went back to my office and got my purse and computer, walked to the elevator, got on the elevator, went to the bottom floor, walked to the parking lot, and got in my car—but honestly, I don't remember any of it. The next thing I knew, I was sitting at the red light heading toward the freeway and trying to compose myself. I needed to call my husband and tell him what happened.

I'd gone from excited to angry to extremely hurt. I'd worked so hard on behalf of the chief. I had done everything he asked me and more. He said himself that I performed at a higher level than he could have imagined. For all that, I got no choice, no options, no discussion. Previous people in my position had input on their replacements when they were leaving, but he never asked me who I thought would be a good fit. All the people before me were white men. An African American person had never held that position—one of prestige, hard work, and power.

When I called my husband, he was upset, but he was also working directly for the chief. He was between a rock and a hard place—and probably intentionally, the way the social chessboard runs in these agencies.

What was I going to do? Take HRD? Take the pay cut so close to retirement? Fuck that!

I hit rock bottom, but I kept my dignity. I decided to retire. The news was so shocking that even newspapers wrote about my groundbreaking career and my early, "abrupt" retirement.

It was clear to me—and everyone who'd been paying a damn bit of attention—that what had happened was about one thing and one thing only. No matter how groundbreaking my career had been, there was something I couldn't break: the cement ceiling for women in this profession. I'd hit it, and it was time to go.

REWIND: THE DECISION OF A LIFETIME

Growing up, I didn't have a close relationship with my father. He died of alcoholism when I was an adult, and we didn't even know he'd died until a week later. Every once in a while, he'd send me an email to say he was driving between California and Nevada and looking for me on the highway to see if I was working there as a trooper…which was weird because I work in Washington. I knew him as well as one could know an alcoholic. When I was younger, I was close with my mom. I love her, and she taught me many things I still carry with me—like how to have good manners and how to speak correctly. However, as I got older—as it happens sometimes—we grew apart. So, when people talk about being close to their parents, I still wonder what that feels like.

I share this with you so you can understand how my journey started. I didn't have a lot of adult role models—except for a woman I met while I was working at the donut shop. Her name was Vernestine, and she was as classy and as fabulous as they come. Her hair was neat. She always smelled good. And the smocks she wore to her job at a local grocery store were always pressed. She had a presence, and I was struck by that.

At her insistence (because it had better benefits), I left the donut shop and went to work at the same grocery store as Vernestine. I was a bag girl, and she was a checker. During these shifts, I got a ton of advice—some unsolicited. I liked it, though, because I wasn't used to that. There weren't a lot of people who could tell me what to do, but she was one of them. She was fearless. A powerhouse who invested time into helping me grow. When Vernestine spoke, I listened.

Vernestine is the reason I went to college. She pushed me to be better.

"You're smart," she told me. "There are things you can do that I couldn't do. So go do them."

Vernestine taught me to be strong and hang in there. She'd say, "You have to grind up your ass and stay and get this thing done." Who knows what that means, exactly, but I understood what she was saying. You have to persevere through the hard times. You can't just lie down and give up the second you get hurt. I took that message to heart, and I carried it with me.

Vernestine rooted for me. When I came home from college without my degree—the same one she had pushed me to attend—I was broke and ashamed. I had to live in my car and couch-surf with my friends. I needed a job, and Vernestine knew it. She marched into the manager's office at my old grocery store job and *told* him he was going to hire me back, because I was a good employee. Next thing I knew, he called asking me to come back to work. She would take on anything—she was an army of one. I learned from her how to draw strength despite lacking resources. She didn't have many herself, but she kept punching her way out. She was a single mom—as I would become later in life—and she wasn't afraid of anything.

I wanted to be like her. And I think I did a pretty good job, all said and done.

Felicia, my best friend in the whole wide world, was another huge point of support in my life at that time—and she has been since. Years later, she'd help me survive the academy, sending me mail, cookies, and words of encouragement. In the years after that, she has stood by me through marriage, childbirth, divorce, another marriage, and a host of other things in my life. She and Vernestine are pillars in my life and core to who I am today.

When I decided to join the WSP, I didn't tell everyone on purpose. The few people I did tell thought I shouldn't join because they said the patrol was racist and against African American people and they did not like women. They said I wouldn't get hired.

I didn't come to the decision lightly. I'd looked at several agencies, including the LAPD and Las Vegas Metro. I went on a ride-along in Las Vegas but just didn't get the right feeling. I also went on a couple of rides with the Seattle Police Department, but it wasn't a good fit for me.

Then, I went on a ride-along with the WSP. I realized they still might not be my people, but they could be my *agency*. They were clean, disciplined, and sharp. They kept their cars clean. I was coming from United Airlines, which catered to the business population, so I was used to everything being in order. The WSP was a well-respected organization, and I was going to join them!

I trusted my ability. They asked for extra documents, such as my high school records. I went to school in Pasadena, so I flew down, got my sealed copy of the transcript, and brought it back to them immediately instead of having to wait for two weeks for it to arrive in the mail. It took three and a half months to get hired, which people say was not a long process. Once I was hired, some people said I only got hired because I was an African American woman. It's like they couldn't make up their minds: did they only hire me because I was an African American woman, or did they try to avoid hiring me for that same reason?

I didn't give a shit either way. I had a job to do. I had to tune out all the noise and different opinions that had no real impact on me or what I wanted. If I'd listened to everyone else, I would have sat around doing nothing or stayed at an airline with a terrible retirement plan. I might have lost custody of my son because I had to be away so much to fly. The outcome of my life depended on my perseverance.

If you're deciding which career path will be the best fit, I recommend making a list of what you're looking for. I thought about what I wanted out of the agency. I also had to assess what I had to offer the WSP. The WSP would pay for me to go to college and then give me a 4 percent raise once I had my degree. I hated saying I'd dropped out of college—it felt worse to me than never having gone at all—so I wanted to finish. They'd give me a car to take home, so I'd start work in my driveway, cutting out the commute and giving me more time with my son. They paid for the uniform. As a single mother, this was important. I also didn't want to go on a large number of domestic violence calls, because I knew they would wear me down. Pulling people over on the freeway, I was less likely to run into such situations. Yes, there are "rolling domestics," when someone assaults another person in the car, but those don't happen nearly as often as when you're a city or county police officer responding to incidents in homes.

Of course, there was some truth to what people had told me to discourage me from applying regarding racism, sexism, and other biases. Still, I trusted myself and knew I was strong enough to rise to the challenge. It was also important to me to take the sergeant exam, a story I'll share with you in the next chapter. There were only three African American women before me, and the agency chased two of them away and fired the third, all within a couple of years of joining. I heard their stories over and over again, but I knew I wasn't them. Someone had to challenge the system and create change from within. If no one takes the beating and survives it, then the beatings just keep happening.

The WSP offered me so many good opportunities if I could just stick it out. I felt I needed to get through the challenges and survive. There was money to be made, promotions to be had, and community members to meet. The patrol claims to pay equally, but they get away with unequal pay by doling out unequal promotions. If women make less on average than men, then the agency blames it on their not being promoted to chief, for instance. I wanted to seize the opportunities available to me, despite the unofficial discrimination. Even if people opposed me within the agency, I knew someone would have my back.

Ultimately, I decided I was the boss of my own life, and I took the next step with my whole heart. Even then, though, I've always given myself permission to change my mind. The first decision was to become a part of law enforcement. Check! Then, I had to decide which agency was right for me. Check! From there, I had to chart the best path based on the opportunities and challenges I encountered—and I encountered a lot of both over twenty-three years (and counting).

MY JOURNEY AS A
PUBLIC INFORMATION OFFICER

When I originally started college, I was a communications major. I wanted to be Barbara Walters and have my own TV show. I wanted to be a hard-hitting journalist, not just a news reporter. I wanted to tell a good story and highlight important issues. Then, I had to drop out of school because I couldn't afford to get the degree. It was humiliating.

Once I was in the academy and they asked me what I wanted to do, I said I wanted to be the spokesperson for the state patrol, because our stories needed to be told. We were a good agency, and I knew cops couldn't always effectively talk to the media. (Side note: In college, I had a communications internship, and once I got an invitation to be a ringside wrestler interviewer. I got all dressed up like Barbara Walters, but it turned out the arena for the WWE wrestling was basically a dirt-floored barn. The wrestlers would come out with their dramatic schtick, and I'd ask some stupid question just to get them started. My troopers found that story hilarious when they came across it online: Monica Hunter, the wrestling reporter.)

All told, I felt like I had experience in communications that would make me a good public information officer. I applied and got the job, knowing some people wouldn't be happy. But I was living my life and doing what I thought was best for me and in service of the agency. They needed someone with my energy who could promote a better image than the stereotypes. I held the position for three and a half years and received criticism like you would not believe.

About six months into it, people started to realize I was good. I got offered a job as a traffic reporter, so my Barbara Walters dream turned into me reporting on traffic in uniform. The state patrol worked out a deal with the TV station to pay me for overtime, the use of the car, and the use of my uniform, all of which was expensive. Every night between 5:00 and 6:30, I'd give a traffic update every fifteen minutes. Through that exposure, suddenly every officer in the agency knew who I was. More important to me, though, was that I helped humanize the agency to the community. It has always been about the community. It even got to the point that planners would specifically request me to give returning service members refreshers on U.S. traffic laws. Why? They'd seen me on TV and thought I'd be funny and engaging.

And I was, I think. I certainly wasn't afraid to tell those soldiers I'd arrest them for a DUI and didn't mind throwing their asses in jail, which could ruin their careers. I spoke on the military base for that training as well as for other events, such as for Women's History Month or Black History Month. I loved talking with the people we were sworn to serve.

It was more than something I loved, though. It mattered on a bigger scale.

People could get to know me and see me joke and laugh with the newscasters like a regular human being. As a result, I could serve as a positive representative of cops as well as the African American community. Taking that job allowed me to make an impact in multiple ways.

I also thought about my son and how he'd be proud of me if I did well—so I had to succeed. To this day, Spencer is extremely proud of me, which was my number one goal. I wanted this young man to be able to look up to his mom.

It can feel like a heavy responsibility to need to set an example for so many people and live up to the highest expectations as an African American person, a woman, and a cop. I remember talking to a white woman officer who was tough in her own right. Through that conversation, though, she realized that she could stop being a cop any time she wanted, but I could never stop being African

American. She said she dressed down to shop at Nordstrom just so the clerks would leave her alone, but I told her I dressed up everywhere I went in order to get any level of service and not be followed. It can be exhausting, no question. As we spoke, she began to cry as she realized her own privilege.

It's also rejuvenating and exhilarating to know I have the energy and opportunity to help people and make a difference in this arena. That knowledge is powerful, especially when combined with compassion and humanity.

My career path felt like opening a nesting doll. Each new opportunity contained another. I believe you need to take those chances, regardless of what other people say, in order to keep making progress and following the path best for you.

I got into law enforcement to serve the public. As a public information officer and then with the TV platform, I found people weren't afraid to call me. People I pulled over would recognize me and call me by name. The friendliness and goodwill in the community helped me do my job better, even as people inside the patrol were not as nice to me. The public embraced me and treated me well. I got cards, notes, and emails of support and congratulations from outside the agency when I got promoted to sergeant, even while actual troopers weren't celebrating me.

KOMO-TV and anchors—specifically Dan Lewis and Kathy Goertzen—celebrated me on the air when I walked into the newsroom. I'd taken three months off from my traffic reporting at KOMO to study for the sergeant exam. I'd been working there for three years by then, and they told me just to promise I'd come back. The day the list came out for my promotion, I walked into the newsroom to a standing ovation. I lived in two very different worlds simultaneously: inside, I fought to be relevant and respected, and outside, I got nothing but support and love.

REFLECTIONS ON
THE BOOKENDS OF A CAREER

As I reflect on how my career began and how I was forced into retirement, I become emotional. Retrospectively, I realize that sometimes I went against the grain over the years, and not even on purpose—I simply lived by my values and played by the rules. I didn't ask for special treatment; I simply reached out and grabbed what was there for me to live a good life. Because I followed my own path, I take responsibility for the good and the bad—a side effect of trusting yourself, which we'll cover in the next chapter.

At the end of the day, all of the hard parts made the good ones that much sweeter.

2

Trusting Myself

"Hey, is that your dad's car?" I heard Spencer's friend ask. It was a warm day, and the two eight-year-olds were outside playing.

As state troopers, we drove "take home" cars, meaning our vehicles were our responsibility. The patrol car in the driveway, then, became a conversation piece. I listened to the boys talk outside, curious how my son would respond. It was obvious that the assumption from his very innocent little friend was that if there was a police car in the driveway, it must belong to the "man of the house."

"Nope," Spencer said, his voice proud. "That's my mom's patrol car."

* * *

After I placed first on the sergeant exam, a number of hurtful events took place. One trooper went so far as to write a disgruntled letter that was posted to the Troopers Association website. To this day, it is difficult for me to read.

The anonymous author posted what was essentially a page and a half about my lack of capability to be a sergeant. It was a litany of personal attacks, and the union decided to post it for everyone to read on what was supposed to be a professional forum.

When the letter came out, I didn't see it right away because I wasn't involved with the union. The union had already failed me in the past. When I first came out of the academy, a union leader said that women had been molested at an all-female conference. It was something that felt like a hushed fact, but I wasn't about to let it go. I assumed it was a ploy to spread doubt upon lesbian officers, but I didn't know for sure. What I *did* know was that if there had been sexual misconduct, we should investigate it. We were law enforcement, after all. When I heard that comment, I didn't let it slide. I pushed and asked for an investigation.

It turned out that the claims were unfounded. My request for an investigation got media attention, though, and got the accuser in trouble. This led to backlash against me for not maintaining silence. So, I separated myself from the association. I don't regret blowing the whistle on the person who was involved, because the behavior was unacceptable.

In other words, I already had a strike against me with the union—for doing the right thing.

Then a friend called and said they hated to tell me, but there was a letter about me on the association website. I was in my patrol car, and I drove all the way to Olympia. I called the president of the association and told him I was on my way. I told the president if the letter wasn't down by the time I got there, I was getting damages for defamation. He said he'd take it down.

I didn't read the whole letter at the time (too painful), but the chief and other executive members of the chief's staff did. They said I couldn't worry myself with those kinds of issues, which was easy for them to say. It was one more humiliation. People were speaking poorly about me when I wasn't around. Even if they didn't think the letter was right, they also wouldn't stand up and say it was wrong. I told the executive team such behavior was completely unacceptable, but they wouldn't do anything. As a result, I hired an attorney, because the agency was complicit. The attorney said I was a public figure with plenty of evidence, but once I sued the agency, I'd have to leave. I wouldn't be able to work there anymore. I was not willing to give up the career I worked so hard for, so I decided not to pursue the case.

Instead of suing, I decided to fight from within and make their lives miserable through my success. I found the depths of my stubbornness and decided to stick it out and keep getting promoted. Another one of those grind up your ass moments.

After I retired, I read the letter in its entirety multiple times, and thinking about it frustrates me to this day. However, the silver lining was I also found a letter from the union president ordering the vice president to take the original post off the website. He said he'd always been a supporter of me, believed I would be a good leader, and thought everyone had to give me a chance. Once I found that message in 2019, I sent him an email to thank him for his support all those years before. I said I hadn't seen it at the time but appreciated him speaking up even though it wasn't popular. The original trooper who wrote the letter defaming me claimed he wasn't a racist because he could point to some individual minority in his life, as if that relationship excused anything. He also did not sign his letter.

The experience was pivotal for me. I had to decide whether to leave the agency and my career to fight them from outside or just stick with my plan and fight my way through. I ultimately decided to stay, because the letter emphasized there was even more deep-seated prejudice in the organization than I'd originally thought, despite all the microaggressions I'd already endured. The agency needed to change more than I'd imagined. By staying and not letting the negative treatment dissuade me, I could make an essential impact.

When people try to push you out of an organization that hard, it's because they fear your presence will create change. It was completely ridiculous for the organization to have no African American women except for me. It wasn't 1961; it was 1996. People had been talking about reform for years but not taking any concrete action. I wanted to be a part of the change.

The letter was only one piece of what happened after I ranked first on the sergeant exam. After my highly coveted and difficult accomplishment—my entire unit congratulated me by unanimously, and very publicly, requesting a transfer out of my unit.

They sent an officer who was a former classmate of mine into my office to break the news. We'd attended the academy together.

"You know, Monica," he said. "The guys and I have all talked, and we've all decided we're going to put our transfers in. It's nothing personal, but we just don't think you're going to be someone who can supervise us properly."

But it was, of course, personal. And it had been since the beginning.

From when I first took the sergeant exam, people started chattering without talking to me first. It was extremely hurtful, and I wondered how I would succeed when so many people and factors were actively working against me. A couple of times, I felt like I'd reached the last straw. I'd worked so hard to earn a spot at the top of the state patrol sergeant's list. It was so competitive, and there were so many people who wanted my spot at the top. I'd sacrificed too much to give up easily. So to a significant degree, I simply wrote off the detractors as immature.

The reaction was an intentional form of public humiliation, designed to make me feel uncomfortable and fail. Instead of rallying to help me, "my team" aimed to shame and humiliate.

After I learned of their request, I simply asked him to tell me how I could help them get those transfers out as soon as possible. I knew the state patrol would not allow me to come to work every day and draw that salary with no one to supervise, so the sooner I got them out, the sooner I could get my new crew. I told him to tell me how to expedite the process and asked if there was anything else. I was most certainly not crying and begging him not to go. There was no way I'd feed into their game. He said there was nothing else, and he left.

I asked my lieutenant if he knew everyone was transferring out of my crew, and he said essentially yes, but that "boys will be boys." I couldn't worry about such behavior, even though such a mass exodus never happens. The only person who did not put in for a transfer was the most junior trooper in the crew who was only a couple of months out of the academy. He was quiet, but he refused to sign on with the group, which is an unusual break from the culture of going along to get along. He risked being ostracized to stay on my team, and I've never forgotten that.

I trusted myself enough to know I would prevail in the end, so I told the rest to go ahead and leave, ASAP. I was going to do good work with the department and be a good leader. The departures would have actually offered a clean start. I understood what it took to support people and help them have a better career. The departing officers might have been afraid of my leadership, but I wasn't afraid.

As it turned out, when their transfers came in, the entire group said they wanted to stay. They turned down the new offers, even though I said they should celebrate. What they didn't know was that I'd put in for a transfer of my own. When it came through after six months, I had the chance to tell them I was leaving, but I made sure to say that it was nothing personal.

By that point, they liked me, and even the meanest officer on the team had become my advocate and wanted me to stay. He'd stick up for me and talk about what a good job I'd done pulling the crew together. What he said carried weight because he did not give compliments very often.

When my transfer came through and I went to South Seattle, the number of transfer requests wanting to join my new team was fourteen deep, but there was no room. Why? Because nobody was leaving. My new crew was phenomenal. They were so happy I was there, and they treated me with respect and gave me a chance to be successful. Within six months, it was all good. Even though I'd turned the old crew around in my favor, it was good to close that door, move on, and work closer to where I lived and with people who wanted me to succeed.

As a result, I got to work the beat where I'd started as a trooper. I'd always wanted to go back to South Seattle. There wasn't an opening at the time of my promotion, so I put in my time and waited for the transfer to come through. I trusted my gut, stayed true to myself, and focused on doing good work. It paid off.

"NO CAR FOR YOU!"

Like the group transfer request, not being assigned a car was another form of intentional humiliation after my promotion. As context, when you get promoted, depending on where you are on the list, you have more choices. Traditionally, if you place number one on the sergeant exam, the chief calls you the night before the list comes out to congratulate you. I wasn't home, so I missed the call. I received a message from the chief's secretary saying the chief would like to talk to me, but when I called back, there was no answer. It just rang and rang.

I told my friends I was worried about having missed the call. I was a public information officer at the time, and in that role, you are only as good as your last quote. If the chief was calling, I feared I had said or done something wrong. One of my friends agreed to call around to find out what was going on and call me back. When she did finally call, she told me to wait by the phone.

"The chief is going to call you," she told me.

I waited patiently for it to ring. When it finally did, he congratulated me for placing first on the test.

I was so excited I started jumping up and down and crying, to the point Spencer got scared because he thought something was wrong.

"Mommy came out number one on the sergeant's list!" I couldn't stop saying it, full of joy. Then, Spencer got excited and told me I'd done a good job. I took the time to celebrate because I knew other people weren't going to celebrate for me.

Since the list was coming out the next morning, I was supposed to keep it to myself and let everyone be surprised. When we arrived for a meeting the next morning, someone whispered to me he'd heard I was number one, but I didn't say anything or even turn around. I felt nervous because that person didn't congratulate me. It felt as if he wanted me to know he was aware of my accomplishment—but not in a positive way. I did receive a few congratulatory messages that day, but it wasn't as celebratory an atmosphere as I had witnessed for other people.

Before your first day reporting to your new crew as sergeant, you go get your new badges, turn in your old car, and get a new car. Keep in mind, I was the first one to be promoted. However, when I went down to get my car, the fleet manager said they didn't have one for me. I said there must be some mistake because I was getting promoted. Trooper cars have a light bar on top and a lightning bolt on the side. Sergeants' cars are colored and unmarked, so people know you're a sergeant when you arrive on the scene.

"There must be some mistake," I told him. "Why wouldn't I have a car?"

"I'm not sure." That was the only answer I got.

I went back and told my lieutenant what happened.

"Interesting," he said. "Well, you could always take the light bar off of your trooper car."

"Soooo…I don't get a car?" I asked again.

At that point, the troopers had already told me they weren't going to work for me and were transferring out, so it was my second humiliating moment after the exam. I had to take my new license plate and put it on my old trooper car, which I've never seen happen to anyone else—before or since.

But I kept going.

COMMUNICATION

People wanted to come work for me because I quickly gained a reputation for having good communication and management skills. Most of all, I showed up. I came to work every day. I balanced my schedule between working the road and getting my paperwork done. My door was always open. People would come in and know I was interested in what they wanted to do. Some of my first meetings with my crew focused on what they wanted for the future and how I could help them get there.

Did they want to work the road forever, or did they want to pursue becoming a detective or some other specialty position? There are many different opportunities in the agency, and I wanted them to think about their longer-term plans so I could help them chart a path toward their goals.

They said no one had ever asked them such questions before. I took the same approach with every crew, even while they were treating me poorly. I showed up for work every day no matter how sick and tired I was, and I would not let them see my frustration. I would help them anyway, and eventually I made progress. They saw I was a hard worker who actually went in the field with my people. They saw I was good at arresting drunks. I helped them, side by side, and doing so quickly turned the atmosphere around.

I never changed who I was or bent to the will or pressure of the naysayers. I trusted that I knew what was right in my core, and I knew I was strong enough to remain on the good side of history.

QUALIFYING WITH A WEAPON

Though I've shared a couple of stories about my success and strength as a trooper and a leader, I wasn't naturally good at everything that comes with being in law enforcement. Far from it. In fact, at first, I was very uncomfortable with a gun. I'm a city girl, and the only people who had guns where I grew up were gangbangers and criminals. Though I approached the academy with the mindset I could do anything and was comfortable confronting people all day long, having a gun was still scary.

My first time on the range, the instructor taught us everything about the gun—how to load it, how to know when it's live, and so on. There was a lot to remember. Most of the people in my class had been hunting since they were kids or came from military or police families, so guns weren't a big deal to them, even among the women.

The instructor said women normally shoot better than men for some reason, but that was not the case for me. I was not hitting the target. I felt freaked out, anticipating the recoil. I'd move the gun before pulling the trigger. In the process of launching the bullet, I'd miss my target.

Not center mass…the whole target.

I thought, *What is wrong with me?* The instructors had looks on their faces like, *Oh, Jesus. Here we go.*

Every time we went to the range, I could feel myself shaking and a pit would form in my stomach. It reminded me of the way so many people say they feel about public speaking or going to the dentist's office. At that time, I'd have preferred to go on stage in front of 100,000 people than to shoot that damn gun again.

Other people loved range day—it was fun for them. I, on the other hand, got more and more anxious. I'd hear the command, pull the trigger, and not hit the silhouette.

There started to be a conversation that I wasn't going to make it through the academy because my skills weren't improving. The deck was already stacked against me: I was the only African American female in the class, I was older than most of the people around me, and I had been a flight attendant before making the career switch. To say I was an anomaly to the regular world of troopers would be an understatement. To their credit, the state patrol instructors did give me special permission to take my firearm home on the weekend to practice since I didn't own one. It was the only way I could improve.

As word got around, a trooper named Karen DeWitt left a note for me at the front desk at the academy. She didn't talk to me, but the note said she'd heard I was struggling with firearms. Her act of kindness was truly a godsend. I'm still in touch with her. It took effort for her to care that much about the career of someone she didn't know. She had simply heard about my situation and wanted to help.

The note gave me the name of a firearm instructor she said was "one of the best in the world." His name was Roy Leopard.

I called Roy. We had to meet on the weekend because he was located almost an hour from my house, and during the week, I—like all trooper cadets—was required to live at the academy. I didn't care, though. I was willing to do whatever it took, and I wouldn't accept failure. For all I knew, at first, he could have been the Hillside Strangler. My mind was on accomplishing the goal.

Luckily, Roy would turn out to be one of the kindest people I've ever met, even to this day.

I found someone to watch my son for a few hours, and I drove out to Roy's house. He was in his mid to late sixties. My first day there, he put some stones in my hand—the kind that change color. He told me to keep my hand closed.

"Tell me why you're here and how I can help," he said. I explained everything—how much I needed this to work for me and my son, how nervous I got with the gun in my hand, how much pressure I'd put on myself to get this right.

He listened. When I was finished, he asked me to open my hand.

"Look at the stones now," he said in a strong, grandfatherly voice I'd come to appreciate. The guy had more guns than a gun shop, but he was so sweet and multi-faceted. "Ah, those aren't the calm color. I know I can help you, but we need to help you calm down first."

This became our ritual: I'd walk in the door, and he'd give me those stones.

"Let's see where you are," he'd say. "Let's talk."

And we did.

By the third visit, the stones would become the right color much faster. And then, we'd get to work.

His approach was much more understanding, like learning how to shoot from my grandfather. Roy was a good person. At the academy, I couldn't say I felt afraid of the gun. I couldn't let people think I might fail. With him, though, I could be vulnerable so we could get to the root of the problem and he could help me.

He said my fear was normal, and he validated that guns can be scary if you don't know how they operate, if you don't slow down around them, and if you don't have experience with them. I met with him every single weekend. We started in his garage with an airsoft pistol and the target. Then, we went out into the middle of the woods. We'd shoot at random things: bottles, old freezers, or whatever we found out there, and I became more and more comfortable with the firearm.

I'm grateful for Karen, the woman who wrote the note, and for Roy. What would have happened if I'd never gotten the chance to work with him? The academy sure wasn't going to refer me to someone like him. For all they knew, he could have killed me and put me in a refrigerator, and it would have been months before anyone found me. It turns out that Roy was an angel and did so much for me and my son.

Eventually, I had one last chance to qualify. My firearm instructor and a couple of other officials explained to me that if I didn't qualify that day, I'd have to leave the academy.

"With all due respect," I told them, "I'm not leaving. I can't. That's not an option."

By the looks on their faces, they didn't hear that response often.

I couldn't leave because I was going through a divorce. My son, Spencer, was four years old. I had responsibilities. I knew I had to get qualified that day. We went down to the range, and there was a group of people prepared to watch me and two other cadets attempt to qualify, which made me that much more nervous. They were behind me as I shot downrange.

In the end, I qualified and felt so relieved to succeed. When I went back to class, my classmates were genuinely happy for me. They'd wanted me to make it. I was able to save my target from my qualification, and I mailed it to Roy and thanked him for all his help. I wanted to pay him, but he wouldn't let me…which I appreciated because money was short.

For graduation, we drove our cars from the academy, which is in Shelton, to the capitol rotunda in Olympia. When I came out of graduation, I found Roy had framed my target and left it on the push bars of my patrol car. He was standing not far from my patrol car near a tree. He had attended graduation. I went over to him, and we had a moment and talked about how exciting it was. I expressed my deep gratitude and explained I would not be there without him. For probably five years after I graduated, every year, he'd bring me a big batch of delicious homemade chocolate peanut butter balls and leave them at the district office. I looked forward to them, and he knew it.

Roy ended up having a stroke and eventually passed away. To this day, I know I wouldn't have made it without his help. He gave me a giant pep talk about believing in who I was and trusting myself.

He knew I could do it and that my fear came from the state patrol bullying me, pushing me around, and yelling at me. I couldn't operate under those circumstances when I was still building my skills. He helped me tap into my belief I could succeed, and he stayed with me until I actually did it.

You see a lot of negatives in this line of work, but Roy is an example of the opposite of that. Of people believing in other people. He was a mentor when I needed it most.

THE VALUE OF MENTORSHIP

If you're interested in pursuing law enforcement, I highly recommend finding a mentor like Roy was to me. There are people out there who are willing to help. When we keep our pain and fear all to ourselves, no one can help us because they don't know what's going on. You have to find the right space to be vulnerable. I couldn't tell my instructors how scared I was because they would have questioned my ability to be a cop. The level of emotional immaturity that sometimes exists in the world of law enforcement inhibits that kind of open communication.

We have to know ourselves and then be open to receiving help. If we are, then people can respond to us. If we try to handle everything on our own, we're liable to collapse and quit. Had I given up, I wouldn't be here—and let me tell you, throughout it all, I like being here.

For all the aspects of law enforcement being a good old boys' club, there's a moment of light in every single dark space, no matter how small. Even the tiniest pinhole is enough to see possibilities, and I can increase the light from there. I searched for it.

OWNING BOTH SUCCESS AND FAILURE

The value of trusting yourself is you get to live your own life. You will be responsible for everything you earn and for both your successes and your failures. If you stumble, you get back up instead of lying on the ground and feeling sorry for yourself. As Vernestine said, "Grind up your ass and get going!"

If there's anything I've learned over the years, it's that you can't count on people to celebrate with you, and you especially can't count on them to come save you when you're down. I learned to be the kind of person who could be vulnerable in a way that wasn't weak, but human. And I've never waited on anybody to save me. They were never coming anyway, and I'm stronger for it.

3

Listening First, Not Fighting First

"How long has he been skating?" the daycare worker asked me, smiling.

Spencer's daycare had taken a field trip to go ice skating that day, and he had excelled so much that the daycare workers thought he went all the time.

"It was his first time, actually," I responded. Even being as young as he was, from then on, I knew it wouldn't be his last.

Soon after, I took Spencer to the local skating rink, switching from ice to inline speed skating. He loved it. He could not wait for the weekend so he could spend the entire weekend at the skating rink. He skated for hours and never wanted his time there to end.

For years, we spent every weekend at the skating rink. I loved how much fun Spencer had there. He could skate for hours—and he did. I'd stay with him, setting up shop in the concession area to study for the sergeant exam or have meetings.

As Spencer got older, he wanted to join the speed skating team, and he also wanted to work at the rink. When he was twelve, he began asking Mike, the owner, for a job. Mike responded the same way for all the years that Spencer asked repeatedly: he could work there when he was fourteen and entering high school, Mike said, but not before.

The weekend before Spencer was supposed to begin high school, he was at a birthday party. At the party, the kids were taking turns dunking the basketball off of a trampoline. I got a call that I needed to come take Spencer to the emergency room because he might have broken his wrist. When I arrived, there was no question: Spencer's wrist was broken in two places. At the hospital, Spencer was given something for the pain, and a temporary cast was put on his arm.

Though a bit loopy from the medication, when we left the hospital, Spencer insisted on going to see Mike at the skating rink.

"I want Mike to know I am ready to start work immediately. He said when I was fourteen and in high school I could start working there. Monday I start high school, and we had an agreement. I want him to

know I am ready to work." The fact that the job was the first thing he thought of after leaving the hospital reinforced to me how much he loved the sport and being at the rink.

Mike kept his promise, with one exception: Spencer could not work on the skate floor until his cast was off; he'd need to begin in the novelty shop. Spencer was so disappointed. However, a deal was a deal.

Some of the kids on the team also worked at the skating rink, so my son's request to work there didn't feel unusual. But his "why" might have been.

Inline skating is an expensive sport, as the wheels and skates are purchased separately. New wheels are important before each skate meet. On his own, Spencer wanted to work and assist me with the cost of him being on the skating team. Spencer loved working as much as he hated doing schoolwork... but most of all, he wanted to help me. I want to be clear that he didn't need to help financially with skating. I did well with my job at the WSP. I never complained about money. I taught him about saving money and being frugal, sure, but I never wanted him to think I could not afford to take care of him. Spencer also wanted to be independent. Skating on the team and working at the rink until he graduated high school taught him that and so much more.

I was so grateful for Mike and Kate, the owners of Pattison's West. They treated those kids with respect and dignity. When Spencer was there, I knew he was safe. I loved sitting at the skating rink while he skated. As he got older, I knew it would not be as "cool" for his mother to stay. However, even then, the rink was on my beat, so I'd stop and say hi to him while I was working.

The regulars at the skating rink knew me when I walked in. However, anyone who did not know me would hear Spencer say, "That's my mom."

* * *

One of the best BLM protests I saw was in Houston, Texas. I watched it on the news, and during the live broadcast, an African American woman walked over to a white woman and embraced her. They were both crying. Sometimes white people get criticized for not supporting or for trying to be supportive and missing the mark, but that moment was powerful. This African American woman was tremendously appreciative to see white people standing up and caring about people who were different from themselves.

I share this example for a reason. We as cops—and as people—need to listen first, not fight first.

I tried to remind my troopers it's never us versus them. I don't believe in lines of demarcation when it comes to people. It's not the rich versus the poor or the African American versus the white.

We don't all have to hold the exact same goals, but we're all trying to have a better existence. If we're leaving some people behind, we cause problems for everyone.

I'm certainly not perfect. There were times when I had to separate myself from my dad's alcoholism because it was more than I could deal with, and he separated himself from us, too.

Still, I think we have to find our shared humanity. I'm comfortable connecting with the person who's incarcerated. They may be separated from society as a consequence of their actions, but they're still one of us. I won't let anyone separate me from the people because I'm here to serve the people. There are times I have sent people to jail. I know they don't want to go, but it's the consequence they've earned, and I can deliver that consequence with respect. I don't think I'm better than the person being arrested; I'm simply trying to enforce the law to prevent people from being a danger to themselves or others.

People in jail are human, and sometimes those in custody didn't even do anything seriously wrong. They may be in jail because of traffic tickets. They're not all serial killers. We don't have to dehumanize and write people off when they transgress. Unfortunately, the way the law works, once people check the box that they've been incarcerated, they're effectively barred from access to many parts of society, including housing and employment, even after they've served their time.

Treating people as people is a sign of compassion, not weakness. It makes you better at your job, not worse. Some officers think if you don't walk around with your hands in fists, you must be soft. Of course I'm going to protect my life, but I'm also going to protect the lives of others. Sometimes there's no life in danger, but we create the danger. With George Floyd, the officers created the danger. Even if he did pass a counterfeit twenty-dollar bill, which could have been completely unintentional, doing so didn't put anyone in danger.

At the Criminal Justice Training Commission, we talk about not creating jeopardy and then pretending to save the world. Those officers created that situation. If you're truly confident in your abilities, you don't have to throw your weight around. I'm not a martial artist, but I do know that those with black belts don't go around threatening to break everyone's necks. They start from the inside and work to the outside. They exercise discipline and follow through. Part of mastery is humility and being a good person, rather than showing off.

LEARNING TO LISTEN

The video footage makes clear George Floyd was scared. When he was still in his car and had his hands over the steering wheel, the officers were all yelling at him. He was saying he'd been shot before, but no one was listening. When someone says they've been shot before, it is important to listen because that means they're getting agitated over the fear of being harmed again. The officers had the opportunity to de-escalate the situation by listening to him.

They could have said, "Do me a favor—just keep your hands on the steering wheel, and we'll put the guns away. We need to talk to you." Floyd was crying and in a state of panic, but the officers couldn't get out of their own way and help him. As we know, he ended up dead.

I keep returning to this example not only because it sparked—or reinforced—a movement.

Not only because it will live on in history books that are being written right now.

Not only because it personally touched me—as an African American woman, as a cop, as the mother of an African American man who is also a cop. As a human being.

It is for all those reasons…but also because I can't think of a better example of what not to do. Of what happens when we fight first and listen second. This is something I've never believed in, even before Mr. Floyd was murdered.

I brought my listening skills to the state patrol, and they served me well. I'd pull someone over, for example, and they'd be extremely agitated even though I thought I wasn't doing anything besides talking with them. I'd stand there, traffic whizzing by, listening to what people had to say. Then sometimes when I went to talk, they'd cut me off.

I'd simply say, "I listened to you, and now it's my turn."

I'd empathize with their anxiety, express that I understood they didn't get stopped every day, and usually they'd start to calm down a little bit.

It's not pleasant or productive to have a dynamic with someone where they're all jacked up and right on the edge of starting a physical fight. I've learned to read people and their body language. When they start nodding, I know we're getting somewhere. I came with communication tools, but I still continue to sharpen them daily, because they're important to me.

It's very important to note here that listening doesn't always prevent conflict. How could it? Some people come into this world unreasonable and aren't going to change. Sometimes even when you are reasonable, people respond irrationally.

However, starting with listening as the default rather than aggression leads to better results more times than not. It's that simple.

When I was still a cadet on a coaching trip, I was trying to read a guy, and he was not having any part of my communication. My coach was African American, I'm African American, and then we called in a third trooper who was also a large African American man. We were trying to get the arrestee under control and into the backseat of the car, and he was trying to kick out the window. It took three of us restraining his arms and legs, which we term TLC, and he was calling me a "N*gger b*tch."

I didn't meet anger with anger. Finally, he kicked the larger officer one time too many, and the officer said, "If you kick me one more time—" He didn't even have to finish his sentence, and the man stopped. This just goes to show that different approaches work in different situations, and sometimes people want to harm you no matter how calm you are. Still, I stand by listening being the essential first step.

EMOTIONAL MATURITY

I feel so fortunate I came into this profession later in life. By starting in my thirties, I already had life experience under my belt. I was still physically fit and could do what was required, but I also had maturity and emotional intelligence. I suppose I can be thankful

I grew up in such a dysfunctional household because it drove me to get help through therapy. I learned who I was and gained the emotional and mental security to have tools other than physicality and aggression. I could listen to other people, even if they cursed me or called me ugly names, and know their behavior reflected on them rather than me.

People get angry when you arrest them. Who wouldn't? I was fortunate to have my smart best friend in the whole wide world Felicia, who helped me keep my experiences in perspective. She asked me how I'd feel if someone threw me in a patrol car. It might seem all in a day's work to a trooper, but it's a big deal to the person being detained. I continued to reflect and grow as an officer rather than being reactive.

I also listened to police officers and thought about how their treatment of me reflected on them. People disrespecting me portrayed their own immaturity and insecurity. I can understand their perspective when they feel scared or threatened without condoning their violent behavior toward suspects. My role was—and the role of law enforcement of the future should be—to try to be humble, fair, helpful, strong, and a good listener. This is how we make things better, one stop and one conversation at a time.

4

Leaning into Hard Work, Discipline, and Sacrifice

"Mom, what are you doing here?"

Spencer was in high school, and while he loved the social aspect of school and has always been a good person, he struggled to get his work done. It had gotten to the point that I'd become worried about his chances for graduation. I didn't want him to be a "super senior," twenty years old and still trying to graduate, but I also wanted to be supportive and not shake his confidence.

I remembered years before, I'd seen a movie where a teenager's mother had contacted her son's teacher and asked to sit in on class. The plot was pretty standard: her son played basketball, and he needed a certain grade to stay on the team. The mother was at her wits' end, and going to the school humiliated her son enough that he straightened up.

If it worked in the movie, maybe it could work for me. I thought if I took a day off work and sat in Spencer's class, maybe it would either embarrass or shock him enough to change his ways, like in the movie. At that point, I didn't have much to lose. Something had to change.

Spencer's teacher told me I was welcome anytime, so I took her up on that. That day, as the bell rang and students flooded in the hall, I blended in. I could see Spencer walking about five people ahead of me. Unbeknownst to him, we were both on our way to class.

Suddenly, it was as if he could feel my presence. He turned around, and we locked eyes. That's when he asked me what I was doing there.

"I came to sit in on your class," I told him.

"You're…going to sit in on my class?"

"Yes, Spencer. I think it's important. I need to know what's going on because you don't seem to be getting your work done, and you need to get your grades up. Oh, look. Here's your classroom now."

"Wait, Mom, can you pretend to be like a health worker or something?" he asked, as we were headed into a science class.

"We can pretend whatever you want, but you'll know I'm here, and that's what counts."

Just then, a girl ran up and gave Spencer a hug. She seemed happy to see him.

"Hey, who is this?" she asked.

"It's my mom," he replied, as he always did.

"Hi, Spencer's Mom," she said with a giggle.

"Okay, Spencer," I said. "I'm going to go ahead and introduce myself to the teacher and find a place to sit before everybody gets in there."

After a brief discussion with the teacher, I sat down. Soon after, Spencer came in and sat two rows ahead of me. The girl I'd met in the hallway passed by and said, "Bye, Spencer's Mom." And just like that, the health-care worker story was blown.

Spencer's main problem was turning his work in. Otherwise, he was a good student, always polite and kind to his friends and teachers. I watched as he listened quietly to the lesson, though I could hear the murmurs in the room about why I was there. After the bell, as we filed out into the hallway on our way to math class, more kids began to ask questions. *Spencer flat-out told them I was his mom. He did not seem phased or embarrassed one bit that I was there. One of his friends even commented that she liked my boots!*

When we got into the next class, I again introduced myself and sat in the back of the room. Here, I noticed fewer kids were paying attention. Who can learn in this environment? *I wondered. I know Spencer can't.*

Just then, a girl passed him a note. He looked back at me, as he had been the whole class, knowing he was caught.

"Give it back," I told him. "Tell her not to give you any more notes in class. Don't make me tell her." And he did.

When class was over, I connected with the teacher.

"I don't know how you do it," I told her. "With all the noise and talking and distractions. I understand why Spencer isn't learning very well, but I certainly don't blame you. There's only so much you can do as an instructor. This is hard work."

That was the end of my school day, so I told Spencer I was going to leave. Of course, he offered to walk me to the door.

When he got home that day, I hoped my plan had worked—that he'd be embarrassed and start turning things in.

"My friends want to know when you're coming back," he said instead. "They thought you were cool."

"I'm not coming back, Spencer. This is not how I want to spend my vacation time. You're supposed to change your ways, and then I never have to come back again."

"But it was fun having you there," he said.

What is wrong with you? *I thought.* Who wants their mother in class?

Spencer did, apparently. A lot had changed since he was in kindergarten, but not that.

* * *

Now that I'm executive director, I'm really in charge and can make decisions. Before, I was just trying to keep the wheels on, but now the success or failure is mine. I can be creative in my thoughts, and of course, there's also lots of work to do.

COMPLETING MY DEGREE

I take pride in having modeled hard work, discipline, and sacrifice for my son. I decided to go back to school after Spencer graduated from high school. When I went to college straight out of high school, I did it on a wing and a prayer. I simply did not have the money. Every semester, I was scraping funds together to try to pay my tuition.

I worked all kinds of different jobs, including McDonald's, front desk at the dorm I lived in, and the local post office sorting mail, so I was constantly tired. Once, I reached the end of the semester, right before finals, and didn't have the full amount for my dorm payment. The school told me my whole semester would be a wash if I could not make the payment. I called my mom, but all she could do was pray. She had no solutions except to listen to me cry, which felt terrible.

My sister ended up giving me money that she'd saved to buy a car. In exchange, I drove home and gave her my car. I continued for one more semester, but finally, it was all too much. I left with the idea I'd go back one day, but I always hated saying I'd completed "some college." Fairly or not, I felt I sounded like a dropout or a quitter.

When I returned to Pasadena, I enrolled in cosmetology school, got my job back as a grocery cashier (thanks to Vernestine), and eventually got my cosmetology license. From there, I started my new career and opened a hair salon where I was able to create the atmosphere I wanted for my customers. I felt like I was living my best life and loved being creative and artsy. Heck, I could change my hairstyle whenever I wanted.

After living what I thought was my best life for approximately seven years, I saw an ad in *Essence* magazine for United Airlines and decided to apply to be a flight attendant. Though I enjoyed doing hair, I wanted more. I knew that I would never lose the ability to do hair, but I *would* eventually lose the opportunity to explore the world—an opportunity my ancestors didn't have, an opportunity Vernestine didn't have.

Washington State Patrol cadet inspection, 1998

Me and my best friend in the whole wide world, Felicia,

at my trooper graduation, May 1998

Spencer pinning my badge at my sergeant
promotion ceremony, 2003

My sergeant promotion ceremony, 2003

Doing a KOMO News traffic report circa 2004

Johnny and I get promoted to captain, June 2015

My community support at my captain promotion ceremony, June 2015

Representatives Mosbrucker, Orwall, and I at the Detroit
Sexual Assault Kit Summit, September 2016

Representative Mosbrucker and I meeting

with Indigenous leaders in 2018

Johnny and I at my retirement celebration, August 2019

I took the opportunity, and it was a worthwhile decision. I had many new experiences, but eventually I needed a change again—one that would ultimately give me a path to go back to school. I knew I couldn't raise Spencer as a single mother, work full-time, *and* go to school, so I committed to resuming once he graduated. It was important for me to demonstrate to Spencer and myself that I knew how to complete things. He cheered me on.

The education benefit through the state patrol ended up being a great deal. You have to pay the tuition upfront and get reimbursed if you earn at least a C or better in every class. The program saved me the burden of student loans, which I've seen my niece pay for years. I wanted to set myself up to have no excuses and just do what I felt I was supposed to do.

Going back to school was another one of those "grind up your ass" moments. I did what I had to do and didn't complain. Plus, it was genuinely rewarding to go back. It didn't feel nearly as hard as it had before. I had many more life experiences to draw from when we had discussions in class, which made me feel like I had more tools in my belt than my younger self had.

I ended up majoring in political science, even though I'd started in communications in Texas, back when I wanted to be Barbara Walters. I thought I might want to go into politics, but I realized

I didn't after seeing it up close and personal. Mostly, I wanted to learn and finish what I started.

STRUGGLES MAKE YOU STRONGER

I'm an avid sports fan, and I recently watched a viral awards speech by Paige Bueckers at the Espys. Paige is a white woman basketball player, and she talked about wanting to stand behind African American players. She ended by quoting the English soccer player Marcus Rashford, who said your success is in your struggle. Rashford is a handsome player whose mother was a single mom and worked three jobs to take care of their family. He has spoken publicly in the past about how sometimes she didn't eat; she'd say she was full so the kids could have the food. It brought me to tears and was so meaningful. I respect people who rise from difficult origins and then use their platform for positive change. That's a true example of sacrifice.

Some of the same people who talked a lot of shit about me and were very critical of my promotion later came to me for help and mentorship in studying for their own exams. By that time, they'd changed their perception of me. They realized I wasn't a prima donna. In reality, I was a scrappy hard charger. They'd underestimated my survival skills. I can't tell you how hard it was to get divorced, raise my son as a single mother, work as hard as I was working, and have to leave my son with a caregiver and then my soon-to-be-ex on the weekends. I'd already survived my childhood with a drunk dad. People who made assumptions about my strength and character didn't know what they were talking about. I knew, though, it wasn't my place to tell them I could be a good leader—I went ahead and showed them.

I was promoted before the officers who asked me for help studying for their exam, but I knew that they could still end up passing me in promotions. At least I had the opportunity to make sure they knew my philosophy on leadership, my thought process, and how I did business. There's a saying that revenge is like taking poison and hoping someone else dies. I couldn't sit around feeding bitterness, because it would have eaten me up instead of allowing me to progress. It would have been a waste of my time trying to get back at everyone. Instead of staying locked in the damage they caused, I needed to remove the barriers from my own path and keep moving. It's exhausting always to have to prove myself, but it's just another example of where discipline and sacrifice intersect to create opportunities.

LIEUTENANT EXAM

I took the lieutenant exam three times—I didn't have the same rockstar performance as I did on the sergeant exam. The exam presented more of a challenge for me because of its emphasis on writing and administrative skills. I was also in school at the time—a place I'd partly returned to specifically to improve my writing skills. I wanted to transfer to a specialty position in internal affairs, which I knew required writing.

I felt embarrassed by my initial performance, but then I thought, so what? Embarrassment can lead to growth. I kept going. I was in internal affairs at the same time I had final exams before graduation, *and* I took the lieutenant exam. I had so much to do that I figured I'd either do well or horribly on all of it. I never scored as well as I wanted. I wanted to be in at least the top nine, because beyond that level, it's harder to get a promotion. There are only about half as many lieutenant positions as sergeant. The captain is an appointed position. That means at each level, you have to do better if you want to rise in the agency (which also depends on openings due to retirements).

The first time I interviewed for a spot I thought suited me well, I didn't get it. The same happened the second and third time, and the process was exhausting. Each time I got passed over, I felt disappointed because I scored well on the portion of the test that showed I knew the material well.

After each interview, I'd ask the captain in charge of the selection process what I could have done better. Once, I had to chase down one of the captains to get the feedback. He told me I'd missed a point because of my Office of Professional Standards history (OPS). My "OPS history" was a lost and later found pager, but I had the sense I wasn't getting the full story. The person he chose instead had SERIOUS OPS history, but it did not hinder him from being selected. At that time, I realized there was no good oversight or systematic reason for the promotions.

Despite the disappointment, I never got discouraged. I actually felt motivated, knowing someone would have to promote me if I kept coming back. I resolved to continue interviewing, following up, and improving until I got promoted. I felt energized and continued to improve my writing. I knew I was a better employee than some of the other people being promoted, so the truth would come out eventually.

5

Building Bridges

"Do you want to go on a ride-along with me?"

Spencer had always said he wanted to be a trooper, even when he was very young. He'd say, "One day, we're going to patrol together." I loved that he wanted to work with me, but in my mind, I thought, Lord knows that by the time you're old enough to be a trooper, I'll be out of this car. *Not out of law enforcement, per se, but out of that seat.*

Spencer never became a trooper, but by inviting him on a ride-along, we could still have one more shot at "patrolling together."

It was hard to find people to stop that day. Everyone seemed to be on their best behavior! Eventually, I stopped one woman for speeding—only to discover she had a suspended license due to tickets. She broke down when I walked up to the window, and I could tell it was genuine. She said she was trying to get to her workplace, a restaurant, and that this was the only way she could feed her family. Some people cry when they're stopped as an act, but I had true compassion for this woman. I could feel her struggle. I could have had her car impounded, but I didn't because I believed she was doing the very best she could. Later, off-duty, I'd try to find her and give her a little bit of money. But at that moment, as I spoke with her, I was very aware of my son waiting for me in the passenger seat of my patrol car.

He was doing what he always did: watching his mom. Through all the challenges I faced in my career, I never lost sight of that.

* * *

It all started as meetings were wrapping up one Friday afternoon. We were discussing weekend plans, and Chris—a friend and fellow sergeant—mentioned he had a date. I knew he'd broken up with his girlfriend and was trying to get back "out there," but I had my concerns. I'd even briefly mentioned to my husband that night that I thought Chris was struggling a bit and that I was worried about him. I didn't know it then, but later I discovered that others knew he was battling with alcohol addiction, yet they didn't say anything. That feels like cowardice to me. Not the addiction, but the silence—and it would come back to haunt us.

That night, around 4:20 a.m., I got a call from a trooper in South Seattle.

"Somebody just called and ruined my day," he said. "So I'm about to ruin yours."

Well, I was *really* awake then.

"I need you to get up and come to the scene. Chris just high-centered his car," he said. "He's drunk, and he's trying to get us to do something that we shouldn't do."

"Okay, I'm up. I'm up. Let me just get dressed, and I'll be on my way."

My mind was racing. This was my friend—someone who had just been over to my home a few months prior for Thanksgiving and had even stopped in for some dessert on Christmas. I wasn't exactly sure what was going on, but I knew I'd figure it out on the way. I rushed to my patrol car and headed to Pierce County. I'd moved so quickly that I hadn't even gotten an exact location by the time I started driving.

Then, I got another call from the lieutenant.

"He's at his ex-wife's house," he said. "Here's the address. I need you to go conduct a field sobriety test and take him to have a BAC done."

As I changed course, I got more calls—this time from other officers.

"Sarg, where are you? How much longer till you get here?"

They weren't sure what to do. I told them they could leave because I knew where Chris was, and I was on my way there.

Once there, I had to use the garage for a field sobriety test before ultimately putting him—unhandcuffed still—in my patrol car, heading to the station for the BAC test. It was all I could do not to cry in that moment, not just because Chris was my friend, but also because he had kids and responsibilities. I did not know how this would look for his career.

But I had a job to do. I took him to the station, just like I would do with any other DUI. I had to handcuff him then and ask a series of questions for my report.

Several hours later, the lieutenant, Chris, and I went to Chris' home to pick up his car, gun, and badge because he was going to be put on administrative leave. As he went upstairs to get his equipment, I felt nervous: I wondered if all he could see were his life and livelihood slipping away. He's just gone through a bad breakup. He has four children. He just got arrested by his friend. *What if he hurts himself?* I thought. I was afraid for him, so I asked the lieutenant to go upstairs and be with Chris while he gathered his things, just in case. Just as the lieutenant began making his way up the stairs, Chris started coming down them, commission card and equipment in hand.

"Hey," I said. "Are you going to be okay?"

"Yes." That was all he said. We hadn't talked much up to that point, either.

I called him a couple days later to let him know that I was still there for him and that I didn't judge him for what happened. Together with another colleague, Doug, we went to breakfast. Even though I knew I'd done the right thing, I was nervous walking into that restaurant, but I didn't need to be. We hugged, and Chris apologized profusely. He said he was checking into a sobriety facility, and he did.

Later, when I was working for internal affairs, I heard the 911 calls and car audio from that night, and I was shocked. Chris had called several troopers asking for help getting his car uncentered. One, a young trooper from King County, responded. When Chris got into his patrol car, Chris asked again if he'd help push the car so he could keep driving to his destination. The trooper, though young, recognized the huge problem with this.

"No," he'd said. "I'm not going to do that. Get the fuck away from my car!" That trooper sent Chris back to his own vehicle and drove away, calling 911 in the process to report a collision. He did not mention it was a trooper, let alone a sergeant. Apparently, they'd gone through the roster of who could respond. When they got to my name, they stopped.

"You know what? Give me Sergeant Alexander's number. I need her home number," he'd said on the recording. "I need to call her right now. Because she will do something."

He knew Chris and I were very close, but he also knew my integrity would not allow me to ignore what had happened. He didn't feel the other people he was told were available would do anything. The troopers Chris tried to talk into helping him—those who worked directly for him day to day—were really upset by being put in that position.

For me, it was good more than bad. It was bad that I had to respond, but it was good that the troopers trusted me.

Fast forward: Chris got out of rehab and received a suspension, not a demotion. I was sorely disappointed in Chris because of how he had involved his troopers in the situation. In a job that's already demanding, they endured extra discomfort because of their superior's moment of poor judgment.

When Chris came back after the suspension, after everything was said and done, he visited me at my office. I love that we were able to salvage our relationship—in large part due to him understanding the work that I had to do. As of this writing, it's been over ten years since the incident, and he's accomplished so much—including getting his bachelor's and master's, traveling the world and, most importantly, getting and remaining sober! He retired as a respected sergeant, someone who fought addiction and tried hard to change. He still sends me pictures of his sobriety coin and photos from his travels to express gratitude.

This story embodies the difficult truth that sometimes we do hard things not knowing what the outcome is going to be. I didn't know if I was going to lose my friend. I didn't know if my friend was going to try to take his own life. I didn't know if he'd be successful in the DUI program. So many unknowns! What I *did* know was that doing right by our friends, by our troopers, and by our community was (and always will be) more important than making everybody happy.

That's the thing about life and what happens when you treat people well—you *get* to have opportunities to be grateful, even if those opportunities come as a result of conflict or struggle. Doing the right thing is always worth it.

THE FUTURE YOU DESERVE

Self-worth, love, care, and kindness are all essential, and they don't mean weakness. They form my personal foundation, regardless of how other people behave.

Building bridges is hard enough as it is without having to build them between our past and future selves. It's best to get on the high ground and stay there.

I cannot change that I'm an African American woman in a white man's world, and I don't want to. I want to be exactly who I am.

I recently got a call from one of the commissioners who didn't want me to have the job I do now—the one that puts me in charge of the WSCJTC. It's a big, important job…and he knew it. He was adamantly against me, but on that call, he wanted to know how he and others could support me. We had a cordial chat. When I hung up, my executive assistant couldn't believe how professional I was toward him despite everything he'd said and done in the past—but I know I have to work with everyone.

STICKING TO YOUR GUNS

When I got promoted to sergeant, my cohort of troopers congrat- ulated me by unanimously requesting a transfer. There's another part to that story that I haven't told you yet, on purpose. But I will tell you now.

Right before I took my transfer to South Seattle, one of those troopers who didn't think I was good enough to be his leader received a complaint. A woman he'd arrested for driving under the influence said he'd stolen money out of her purse, but he vehemently denied the allegations. I asked the trooper to explain *exactly* what happened with the woman's purse when he arrested her. He explained in detail, and I called the woman and asked if she'd check the last known location of the purse.

"I know sometimes people misplace things when they're intoxicated, and I just want to make sure your property is really missing before I fill out the paperwork," I told her. And I meant it. If a report needed to be filed, I would have been the first to do it. And even though I knew the trooper in question wasn't a fan of mine, that wasn't going to stop me from doing my job and helping get to the bottom of the complaint.

People who are drunk misplace things all the time. I knew this from my father. As I spoke with her, she became upset. I let her talk until she'd exhausted herself. Then, I told her exactly what the trooper told me: that he hadn't taken the money when she was in custody, and that it was instead in a specific location in her purse.

I asked the woman to please go check her purse again and call me back if she couldn't find what she was looking for. When she called back a little later, it was to tell me she'd located her money. We had a cordial conversation, and she was grateful.

The problem ended up being quite simple to resolve, but so few officers know how to communicate effectively. The trooper who was accused had been one of the meanest in the group, but suddenly he became a Monica fan. He ended up telling people what a good leader I was and how I had a great gift for communicating.

I didn't call it "having a great gift." I called it being a human being, doing my job, and building a bridge.

FIGHTING FOR THE LEADERS OF TOMORROW

I built my good reputation brick by brick. I was intentional about not only *how* I led, but *who* I led. In my head, when the new troopers reported to the district office, it was like the NFL Draft! When someone solid graduated, I'd put in my request and fight like crazy to get them in my crew. The two people I got were from different classes and both were amazing. We still talk. One was recently promoted to sergeant, and when she texted to tell me, she said she hoped I'd come back as the chief. She said she learned and grew from having me as a leader and that I helped pave the way for her, which was very kind of her to say.

The other one was promoted to sergeant several years ago. He took the sergeant exam as soon as he was eligible. He choked up while thanking me during his promotion ceremony. I was so touched by their gratitude. Good leaders mentor the younger people coming up, which was always my goal. I wanted to help cultivate new leaders who would continue striving to improve the agency even after I was long gone. I don't take credit for their hard work, but I am honored they allowed me to be a part of their journey. It makes the struggle and challenges feel worthwhile.

I'm the only African American woman ever to retire from the WSP. The others quit. The bridges I've tried to build are so the people walking across behind me will have a better experience. If I do a crappy job, they'll have to build and repair on their own. I understand my work is not just about me but the future of the institution. So how I behaved in and out of uniform was huge to me. The community was watching me, and I knew I could create change from inside, improve community relationships with law enforcement, and encourage a culture of calling each other on bad behavior.

What I learned from these experiences is that good leaders are vulnerable enough to own what they don't know, speak to what they do know, and aren't afraid to apologize when they make mistakes. It's disarming to say sorry, but it's very alarming when people refuse to recognize their mistakes or try to justify them. If you try to justify a wrong, it just makes you more wrong. You look stupid, and everyone can see it. It's like the emperor's new clothes.

You can explain your decision, but also admit you could have made a better one. That example helps people. If you are dismissive instead of taking personal responsibility, then you close the door to being inclusive. If you have questions, approach people who know more than you with dignity and respect. What's in your heart comes out of your mouth whether you want it to or not. People see your character through your words and actions.

PATIENCE, SELF-CONTROL, AND PERSEVERANCE

Want to learn this skill of building bridges for yourself? I'll tell you the truth, as I said in the beginning: it can be hard work. If you're coming up and building bridges in a difficult environment, prepare yourself with the knowledge you're going to have to be very patient. Think before you speak. Letting your temper and your mouth get the better of you will have consequences, especially in a leadership role. Learn when to step away, take a deep breath, and come back with a cooler head. There's nothing wrong with saying, "Hey, can we pick this conversation up tomorrow? I think I need some time to process."

If you get swept up in the craziness and fallouts that happen when tempers and emotions flare, you'll become part of the problem. As a leader, you have more responsibility and accountability, and letting your emotions get the better of you will get you in trouble. If someone challenges you on something, stay calm, shut up, and listen until you get all the facts. Stick to the policies and procedures. Know that the respect you have earned can be fragile; it's a lot easier to lose the respect of your peers and subordinates than it is to earn it.

Even if you're not in an official leadership position and just working with your peers, be a model. Yelling and complaining can lead to sanctions, no matter where you are in your career. (Not to mention the fact that it feels better to be the bigger person.)

This can be easier said than done, and I know that. For example, I was recently working with a recruit who was a witness in a harassment case. She was scared, crying, and thinking about if she was in the right place. I heard her out. I listened—again, that "secret weapon" that isn't really a secret at all.

Then, I told her law enforcement was her career, and it was time to take that career back. I didn't want her to quit. Our profession needs people like her. She'd been in the academy for sixteen weeks and only had three to go, so in my mind, there was no turning back. I told her I could see the bright light at the end of the tunnel, and I wanted her to see it, too.

There, in my office, I shared some of my experiences. I told her she didn't have to let people tell her what she could or couldn't do. I told her that when someone is toxic, she can say what she has to say and then walk away. Everyone doesn't have to love and accept us. We get love from our families and friends, and it's just a bonus if we get love at work—never a requirement.

After she had a good cleansing cry, I encouraged her to stand up straight like she had a rod in her back and go back to work. What I told her goes for you, too, if you're reading this: throughout your career, there will be people who don't accept you. They'll get angry when you do the right thing, which is hard. But you have to get used to that dynamic, and you cannot stop trying just because it's hard. Stay the course *because* it's hard, and you come out stronger. You're the boss of you.

That recruit who thought about giving up graduated three weeks later. Before she left, we spoke briefly, and said she was coming to see me down the line.

"My door is always open," I told her.

And it is—for her, and for all current and future members of law enforcement who want to learn how to do this job with dignity and honor.

REMINDER: YOU ARE NOT YOUR JOB

When we talk about "doing this job right," it's important to make the distinction that what we're doing *is a job*. It is not who we are. This is a simple concept to understand on the surface but one that can be more challenging to internalize. In this profession, especially, that line can feel blurred, and cops can get it confused.

For example, I can introduce myself as a twenty-three-year retired captain of the Washington State Patrol—that's what I did. I wore a uniform for that, and I took it off when I got home. Who I am is Spencer's mother and Johnny's wife. That doesn't come with a uniform. And my African American skin certainly doesn't come with any extra privileges.

That's the difference, and it matters that we understand it.

6

Leveraging My Tenacity

Spencer has always been independent. He enjoyed his job at the skating rink through school and even kept it as a second job after he graduated. Because of the Affordable Care Act, I was able to keep him on my insurance for a brief period of time, but as that drew to a close, I warned him that he should look for a position not only with insurance, but one that could help him learn more about the profession he wanted to pursue: law enforcement. He'd always said he wanted to be a trooper. His first try didn't work out, but I encouraged him to keep taking steps that were closer to that goal. One of those steps was to apply to become a dispatcher.

I knew that being a dispatcher was/is a very hard job because you have to absorb a lot of trauma daily, it doesn't pay nearly enough, and those who perform in that role do not get the credit or attention they deserve. Dispatchers are often forgotten about but are critical to the safety and success of officers. Still, I knew that for Spencer, it would be a great and necessary learning experience.

Once he passed the interview process, background screening, and poly-graph test, he was hired. I was a bit disappointed that he wasn't hired as a trooper like he'd always wanted to be, but at the same time, I was proud to have Spencer working at the WSP. It felt like a family affair: me, Spencer, and Johnny.

When I would call dispatch, my name would flash on the screen. When Spencer was working, he would always try and answer the phone if he saw my name. He would not always beat others to the phone, but he would sure try. Spencer would answer the phone and say, "Hi, Mom!"

"That's Captain Mom to you!" I'd joke. From that point forward, when I called, he'd pick up and say, "Hi, Captain Mom."

After being in dispatch for about a year, he again tested to be a trooper. Though he made it further than he had in his previous attempt, the WSP told him he still wasn't ready. Spencer was discouraged and frustrated. He didn't understand why the WSP would hire him for a communications role but would not hire him as a trooper cadet. I tried to be encouraging, but I didn't have any answers. This was his fight.

Spencer then decided to test at the Tacoma Police Department. He made it to the oral phase and froze in front of the panel. Again, he was disap-pointed in himself. The Tacoma recruiter—a great guy—pulled Spencer outside and gave him a pep talk, telling him to come back and try again.

Pushing forward, Spencer interviewed at another police department and made it all the way to the "meet the chief" phase. However, when he arrived at that meeting, he was told the department had decided against moving him forward. He was heartbroken and confused, wondering if he was good enough to be in this profession.

Spencer then decided to stop trying and took a position at a tire company, which he enjoyed. He felt valued and appreciated, and he liked the owner. Then, the WSP Communications Division asked him to come back to dispatch. He seriously considered it but ultimately decided not to return to the WSP.

However, he still had that nagging feeling that he was supposed to be a police officer.

One day, the Tacoma Police Department recruiter—the one who had told Spencer to try again—called Johnny and asked if Spencer was still interested.

He was. He got off the bench and back in the game, working out, watching his diet, and focusing again on his goals and purpose.

When he tested again with Tacoma, he passed round after round. Finally, he was invited to meet the chief, and he wanted the job more than ever.

A short time later, he got the call. He'd been hired!

He cried joyful tears, and it was wonderful to see him feel such happiness and pride about his accomplishment. His tenacity got him there. He did not let "no" define him. He kept chasing his dream, and he caught it.

His next step was to come to the academy—the same academy where I am executive director.

His first day, it was my turn to cry uncontrollably.

* * *

"So, did Johnny tell you the good news?"

I'd just left a sergeant's promotion exam and had met up with the chief. We were headed to a media event where he was speaking. As I sat in the passenger seat, I wondered what good news he could be talking about. I hadn't heard from Johnny that day.

"I promoted him to assistant chief! He's really earned it," he said. "Johnny loves this agency! He is loyal to me and this agency," the chief said.

I didn't know what to feel in that moment. Many people—including Johnny—believed I was strongly in the running for the role. Johnny said repeatedly, "If anyone has 'earned' the promotion, you have."

But the promotion didn't just go to anyone else. It went to my husband.

Despite my swirling emotions on that car ride, I knew for certain that I was genuinely happy for and proud of him. My husband is a wonderful man who has had a long, successful career in law enforcement. One of his strongest attributes is how he genuinely cares about people and wants them to be successful. Not one to throw the baby out with the bathwater, he is able to motivate people and focus on their strengths. He is personable, too. He'll do push-ups along with the recruits, showing them he can do more than they can and encouraging them to be better. He will not ask anyone to do something he won't do—something he and I have in common in terms of our leadership styles.

But the assistant chief position was a lot of hard work. Johnny would walk through the halls and say, "I don't want to work that hard," and it was passable. It's not a dig at him—it's true of most men in law enforcement. The bars are different. And as the hardest worker out of the group—the first one in, the last one out, the hand-raiser I had been over the years—I felt passed over.

I want to be very clear: it's not that Johnny didn't deserve to be promoted. He certainly did. But the team already had "Johnnys." From my perspective, Johnnys have been promoted in law enforcement for years. I believe the chief didn't feel bad at all about promoting my husband instead of me because, from his vantage point, the move put money in both our pockets. Johnny and I have always said when one of us wins, we both win. And we mean that. This felt different because, in my mind, the WSP needed female leadership at all ranks. At the time, the WSP was approaching 100 years old and had never once promoted a female to the rank of assistant chief. I believed I could do that and, in the process, open the door for other women coming behind me.

Instead of taking that opportunity, the organization kept promoting more of the same type of men. *Good* men—but the same.

I am a HUGE Seattle Seahawks fan. What if Pete Carroll held a press conference and said, "We have one of the best quarterbacks in the entire NFL, so I'm going to draft three or four more just like him!" Would that work? Hell no.

For a team to be successful, you need a variety of approaches and skills. If you have five quarterbacks and no defensive backs or receivers, is your team going to evolve? No, it's not. That's what happens a lot in law enforcement: we keep promoting or are looking for people like us when we should be looking at the bigger picture.

After my conversation with the chief, I congratulated Johnny over the phone. When I got home that night, it was late. He was sitting on the couch with a good friend of ours. When I walked in, the room got quiet. I said hello, chatted for a moment, and then went upstairs to my room and closed the door. A while later, Johnny came up.

"I know you're happy for me. And I know you're upset."

"Yes," I told him. "I am upset. I can't even really talk right now. One thing I haven't sorted out is exactly how I feel, but I do know that I could never *not* be happy for you. I really am."

He was right. Both of those things couldn't have been truer. It was just complicated that they were both true at once.

THE IMPORTANCE
OF STRATEGY AND TIMING

Everyone goes through rough patches, but oftentimes they're even rougher for women and minorities. There are inevitably times when we feel lonely in our professional world and like people don't understand us. This profession is littered with white men. Women and people of color stand out, no matter where we go.

Sometimes, I sit back, keep my mouth shut, and listen to the room, whether a formal meeting or just a lunch table. For example, in Olympia, we had a periodic Strategic Advancement Forum during which captains and most lieutenants would gather to share information. The captains and most of the lieutenants would go out to lunch during these forums, but they had this habit of passing right by my office without inviting me. I don't believe it was intentional; they'd just grab their hats and walk on by.

So I called them out. I didn't even want to go all of the time. However, I did want to be invited just like my male peers.

"Hey, don't do that again!" I told them. I knew I wasn't "one of the boys," and I never wanted to be. I did, however, need to know what was going on in the captain circle—after all, I was a captain.

It became playful banter later on. They'd say, "Don't forget to invite Monica to lunch!" We'd laugh, and I would respond, "That's right! I LIKE LUNCH, TOO!" The approach was intentional on my part. As I evolved in my career, I never shied away from conflict, but I focused more on timing what I said, when I said it, and how I said it to make the biggest impact. I've always taken steps not just for myself, but for the others walking this path behind me.

That was my hard-won tenacity in action…though it shouldn't

have had to be that way. I did deserve that damn invitation all along. Even after retirement, they still invite me to lunch, dinner, and coffee. I feel honored.

Of course, it took years to get to that place. It was easier for me to stand up for myself once I was a captain and had twenty years under my belt. Other times over the years, I learned that if I heard or saw something that wasn't right, it would be more productive if I waited for my opportunity to address it rather than tackling it right away. That took a lot of compromise (building bridges again and again) as well as knowing what was in my own best interest. My advice to you is that, whether you're in law enforcement or not, think before you speak. Consider whether what you say will help or hurt the situation. Sometimes, the best choice is to hold your tongue, hard as doing so may be.

I have always kept in mind what's right for me. It wasn't popular for me to take the sergeant exam at the first opportunity or become a public information officer, for example. Some people thought I must be stupid or lazy and just trying to get off the road as a trooper, but I leaned on my tenacity and knew it was the right choice. I knew how much talent I had, and I held and believed in a clear vision. I took plenty of flack, but I don't regret my decisions. I worked to help the agency grow and improve, and I fostered goodwill in the community. They got to know me and came to better understand what our agency was doing. To this day, I use the tools of communicating information and fostering trust.

Trusting yourself and having no regrets has deep roots in being strategic, and I've leaned on my strategy skills over and over during my career. For example, recently I was advocating for a law enforcement proposal to use a cell phone application to send micro-trainings to officers. Studies show people retain micro-learning sessions better than if we try to teach them everything at once—and, the last thing we want is law enforcement not retaining the de-escalation and communication skills we teach. This tool to help police officers learn, digest, and remember information in small doses only costs $1 million per year. It sounded like a no-brainer to me, but it was a harder pill to swallow for some. There was a bill on the topic during the legislative session, so I made sure to speak on it. I wanted the bill to be top of mind for legislators, so I used all media outlets at my disposal to help get the law passed. Why? Moving the needle is all about being one step ahead and seeing around corners.

I believe there is huge power and importance in being strategic. I know how to wait patiently for just the right moment and sneak up on an issue if I need to in order to achieve the desired outcome. I don't do so for selfish reasons—I'm not trying to acquire anything for myself. In this case, I was strategic to support the training. I knew we needed it, and I knew implementing it would save agencies money and time in the long run because officers would learn better and faster. By remaining strategic and staying rooted in my values, I'm able to look back on my career with pride and without regrets.

Having no regrets is something a lot of people say but that few people mean.

Me? I mean it.

Even though I didn't achieve everything I wanted to, I feel good about my accomplishments and don't regret my choices. None of us ever get everything we want, but we all have the opportunity to remain true to ourselves. In my case, I learned not to make assumptions about how people would react when I had a question or a suggestion. I always brought issues to my superiors' attention. They didn't necessarily grant what I wanted, but at least I didn't regret not speaking up. No one could say later that they wished they'd known what I thought, because I told them. When I became a supervisor, I listened to input so I wouldn't regret having missed opportunities as a leader.

Of course, I'm human. And looking back, there are certainly things I wish I could have done that were simply out of my control. For example, I wanted to go to the FBI academy. I also wanted to go back to school and earn my master's degree. But, based on the demands of the assignments I received from the chief—some of which, such as my time in internal affairs, I valued deeply—I wasn't able to take that level of executive training. I wish that issue had played out differently, but I simply didn't find a way through it. I could go back to school to get my master's degree now, but I'm sixty years old, so I don't see a point in investing the money. But I certainly still have opportunities to pursue! Maybe one day I'll be governor, a position in which people only follow you if they believe in your principles and ability to make them a reality. If I choose that path, I believe my tenacity will get me there.

You can develop that trust within yourself, too, by knowing who you are, what your goals are, and what your drive is. From that foundation, you never give up. You must always be willing to listen—even when people say what you don't want to hear, and even when you have to read between the lines.

SQUEEZING IN

There's a certain familiarity around sameness. Unfortunately, how we grow is not by being around people who are just like us. We grow in unfamiliar, uncharted, uncomfortable territory. When it comes to the WSP, after almost 100 years of sameness, I believe I brought something uncomfortable. I had to make myself Flat Stanley and squeeze my way in using whatever method it took in order to be a part of important conversations. I did that for my future and for the future of law enforcement. I wanted to break that ground for the women who I knew would come behind me.

(And yes, I do like to go to lunch.)

I still get calls from my friends at the WSP, and they ask me to go to lunch, dinner, and coffee. I love that, and I love them. I love that we broke through that uncomfortable space and that, as a result, they are also willing to have uncomfortable conversations.

"Mo, I need to talk to you…"

When one friend in particular calls and leads with this, I know it's about to get real. I know he's about to say some things to me that he might not be comfortable saying to others in this field because he knows I care about him, I care about the agency, and I care about whatever situation he needs to discuss.

And once in a while, that same friend will say, "I love you, Mo," and burst into laughter. That's what happens when you squeeze into the spaces that may or may not be designed for you: you start some much-needed renovation on those spaces, making them more accessible not only to you, but to others.

PROVING MYSELF

My experiences have helped me stand up to pressure. I see my husband now meeting some pressure and resistance. This is new to him because he's never had to prove himself. He walks in the door as a proven commodity because he's tall, handsome, and outgoing. People think he looks great in his uniform and automatically assume he's a great leader. He's a good guy, of course, and I love him. But he rarely has to *prove* that he's a good guy. He's not confrontational, whereas I don't shy away from confrontation. If people want to say something under the radar, I'm not afraid to get everything out in the open, clear the air, and move on.

I compare our approaches to show that, in some ways, constantly proving myself has been good for me. It's a form of cultivating mental strength, like in martial arts. You need physical skills but also psychological toughness. That constant training breeds confidence. I don't pick fights, but if a fight comes to me, I'm ready for it.

All my years as a trooper under those conditions helped sharpen the tools in my toolbox. I like to think of it like I have a box of tools I've collected from all the different people I've interacted with in my life—so many situations, so many challenges, and all of them different. When I need a tool, I pull it out.

You don't use the hammer for everything. Taking that approach is part of what got law enforcement to this point. What you *do* need is a multitude of options and the wisdom to choose the right tool for the right moment.

7

Doing What's Right for the Community

"Dang, Mom. This is hard."

About halfway through his time at the academy, Spencer stopped by my office to talk.

"All I do is eat, sleep, study, and come here. That's it. And I'm not the kind of person who doesn't have to study. I have to study a lot."

"I know, Spencer," I told him. "It's designed to be that way."

He looked me in the eyes then and said something I will never forget.

"You did it with me. I was just a little boy, and you were doing all this plus taking care of me," he said. "What am I complaining about?"

I never forced my struggle on anyone—least of all Spencer—so it was very interesting and rewarding to hear him come to that realization, almost in real time and on his own.

"You were doing this AND being my mom," he said. "If you can do that, I can make it."

And he did.

* * *

When my husband got promoted in 2018, it did give me an unexpected gift: one more session to be a legislative liaison. That session represented the crescendo of my legislative time. I was able to be a part of securing $11 million for a new high-throughput lab to process years—sometimes decades—worth of backlogged rape kits. Kits that had been sitting on shelves all over Washington, untested. Our oldest kit was from 1983, and there was a backlog of 10,000 in total.

This issue was public knowledge because investigative reporters had started uncovering the backlogs across the country. Despite the publicity, there was a major lack of action and overwhelming apathy.

A few of us would not settle for that.

All four years I was the legislative liaison, I worked on the sexual assault issue. (In full disclosure, I was not aware of this problem before I became the legislative liaison.) The high-throughput lab was one of the most important parts because it meant testing the kits. The sexual assault tracking system ensured people who had submitted kits could track where the kits were and not get lost. The trauma-informed interviewing bill helped teach cops how to better investigate and interview sexual assault survivors. It was a nonstop grind through those four years for me to learn about the issues, represent them well, and then work with Washington State Representatives Orwall and Mosbrucker to bring other legislators along.

So while my lack of promotion was a setback because it threw off my retirement plan and my goals for myself, it was also an opportunity. Had I been promoted to assistant chief, I never would have been able to do that work. Part of the beauty of my husband's promotion was that he oversaw the budget section, and he could encourage his people to go through a line-item budget on what it would take to build the lab. The initial price we got was $4 million. In response, we put scientists, the budget people, my husband who oversaw fiscal issues, and the representative from the governor's office on the problem. As a result, I got a line-item budget I could take to every legislator I needed support from during the next session to secure the real amount needed: $11 million.

A gratifying moment was getting the governor's office to back us on securing the $11 million. If something's not in the governor's budget, as a cabinet agency, we can't fight for it. I couldn't testify on a bill if the governor didn't support it. So it was a hugely important step to have the governor's senior policy advisor supporting me in persuading legislators to pass the line-item budget.

Once, I had a fifteen-minute call scheduled with the chair of the Senate Ways and Means Committee, but I ended up getting forty-five minutes. It felt like fate. Washington experienced a major snowstorm, and many of the other meetings were canceled. I was able to explain the issue in much greater detail than I would have been able to otherwise. When it came time to testify, Senator Christine Rolfes knew so much about it that she gave me a softball question that allowed me to encapsulate the major points I wanted to cover. That whole experience felt like an act of God. There was a combination of perseverance and luck, and it wasn't always clear we'd succeed.

I cried when we were able to secure that money. The system had not prioritized rape victims, and we finally had the funds to build a lab and make a meaningful difference in their lives by processing the backlog. Having that capacity also helps encourage victims to come forward and discourages crime.

The old approach in which people knew DNA evidence would

just languish for years and perpetrators might never get caught is done. It doesn't work anymore, thanks to the lab. Thanks to Representatives Orwall, Mosbrucker, and Rolfes! Those ladies are sheroes.

The success is still very emotional for me. So much had to fall into place, and we were up against major odds. I spoke with Representative Orwall recently, and we still reflect on how legislators pushed back on us during that time—some of them were extremely disrespectful and talked to us in a way they never would with men. We took a beating to get that lab, and for a long time, we didn't think it would happen. One senator told us to expect only half the money, but I chose to believe we'd prevail, because we needed all of it.

Many people benefited from the law passing. There's a woman I knew who worked in the state patrol in an administrative position that didn't pay very much. She was going to school because she wanted to work in our crime lab, and I was able to connect with her. Now she's working in one of the newly created positions in the high-throughput lab. The lab is lifting women up in more ways than one, and it's one of the biggest gifts I feel I was able to give to help give the community. The other one—which should not surprise you, by this point—also helps victims who have fallen through the cracks.

FIGHTING FOR MISSING AND MURDERED
INDIGENOUS WOMEN

Representative Gina Mosbrucker—a get-it-done type of legislator who had also worked on the sexual assault kit processing bill—called me one night with an idea. This wasn't unusual.

"Can you work on a project with me?" she asked. "I just had Native American women come into my office, and they said there are hundreds and thousands of missing and murdered Indigenous women out there. Nobody will pay attention to them. I want you on this with me."

"Let me run it by the chief for approval," I told her. "I will let you know as soon as possible."

The next day, the chief gave me his approval, contingent upon one thing: that we went through the Governor's Office of Indian Affairs (GOIA). I reached out to the representative there, but he did not immediately return my calls. One day, I saw him walking near the Capitol, and I ran over to speak with him.

"I've been trying to get a hold of you," I told him, giving him the Reader's Digest version of the problem. "Can we work together on this?"

He agreed, and it went a long way in cutting through the red tape and bringing this initiative forward. That initiative, by the way, stated that the WSP and GOIA would travel around Washington, meeting with Native American communities to figure out the scope of the problem and how to help. We had twelve weeks to complete these meetings, at which point we'd compile a report to present our findings.

Without fail, at each of those meetings, one of the first questions would go like this: "Are you Native American?"

(Spoiler alert: I am not.)

When I said as much, I was always asked where my tribal liaison was. The tribal liaison position is different from that of the role of GOIA. In the patrol, we've always had a liaison—usually a white man who will, once a year, go to the state meeting for tribes (a beautiful event full of music and culture), listen to the governor speak, yet ultimately accomplish very little.

After hearing the "where is your liaison" question several times at different meetings, I went back to Representative Mosbrucker with a suggestion: to have two designated, dedicated tribal liaisons, one for the east side of the state, and one for the west. She loved the idea. Initially, my chief didn't think we had the capacity for it.

I disagreed. Having dedicated liaisons who do more than attend a meeting once a year sounded like an opportunity to learn about treaties, about the people themselves, and possibly even about ourselves as an organization.

To his credit, he listened. I was able to convince him and shared his approval with Representative Mosbrucker, who sponsored the bill requesting two full-time liaisons, which was funded. She said we were doing "God's work," and she got things done fearlessly!

In support of that bill, I created a report summarizing my observations from the listening sessions I attended across our state. Those sessions almost always moved me to tears. The stories of the women and their families have stayed with me—like the young lady who'd dialed 911 right before she went missing, got cut off, and was never heard from again. One story like this is too many, and there are a whole lot more than one. It was amazing to hear what people had to go through just to have someone pay attention to their pain.

As part of my work, I secured the placement of a photo of one missing Native American woman on a truck that traversed Washington's roads, even into Canada, trying to increase exposure of her case and awareness of the issue at large. At its unveiling, someone saged the vehicle, and they wrapped me in a ceremonial blanket as a sign of gratitude.

After I left the WSP, I asked how the families were doing, particularly the ones I'd grown to know. I learned they were angry. The fact that they felt like it was all a publicity stunt broke my heart because I would never exploit someone's pain. I *wanted* that attention to bring exposure to the missing persons cases.

I told the families when I began working with them that I wouldn't be around forever, which is why the dedicated liaisons were so important. Their purpose was to provide consistent, culturally-competent support to these communities—communities who deserve absolutely nothing less.

To this day, Representative Mosbrucker continues to do this important work. While I was writing this book, she sponsored a bill that would allow family members of a deceased Native American to come bless the remains before they are removed—something core to their culture, and something they should have the right to do.

To say I am proud of and support the continuation of work on this issue is an understatement. In fact, working in support of missing and murdered Indigenous women—and the work with the rape kit backlog—are two of the highlights of my entire career. I've met impacted families and heard their stories, which gave me all the energy I needed to fight for these issues. I wanted people to receive justice and not live in fear. That work is part of my legacy and points to the necessity of continuing to fight like hell for progress that impacts real people's lives. I've talked to the families of shooting victims and women who were afraid to go home because their assailant was still at large. These are human issues. Everyone is someone's child, and missing and assaulted people matter and deserve justice.

COMMUNITY IS THE CORE

Serving the community doesn't have to look like big initiatives and legislative wins—though, those are certainly important, and I'm proud of them.

Instead, serving the community can, and should, start with listening to the community—something law enforcement has not been historically successful at. If I were chief for a day, I would ask my community what *they* felt the biggest problems were with the police force. That way, we could solve them together. We shouldn't be telling people how we're going to police them; we should be policing *with* them. This only works if we give people the chance to vocalize what they see as both the problems and the solutions.

By listening, we can figure out whether a situation is getting better or worse, as well as whether our approach is working. We can't police by ourselves. I always tell people if you don't talk to the community, the community will talk to you—but it will be via a bullhorn, standing outside, calling your department a bunch of racist murderers. No one wants to hear those criticisms, but that's what happens if you don't work with your constituents.

One way I connected with my community is that I lived on the same streets they did, whereas many of my fellow officers lived in other cities and suburbs. This caused them to be more disconnected. There are residential neighborhoods with high concentrations of police, whereas I lived near a substation and around regular civilians. I always lived in a nice area, but I didn't fall into the culture of wanting to be surrounded by other cops. Police communities aren't objectively better places to live, but police seem to gravitate toward each other. The other day, my realtor even gave me a gift card for a restaurant owned by a former police officer.

Living around "regular people" makes you more approachable as a part of the community. Neighbors can walk up and have a conversation with you. They might comment on my patrol car or say they saw me on the news. I have always enjoyed knowing my neighbors and having real connections with them, rather than just being in a job enclave.

LISTENING TO SERVE

I once asked a woman to get out of her vehicle and get into mine because she'd been in a collision and her car was going to be towed. She told me she didn't want to. Instead of screaming in her face and demanding she comply, I did something else.

I asked why. Simple as that.

She explained that she was wearing white pants and that the accident had scared her so badly, she'd soiled them. She was embarrassed, and understandably so. There were all kinds of people around, including other troopers. I told her I completely understood and got a blanket for her to wrap herself in to walk to my car with dignity. She wasn't trying to hurt me or be noncompliant; she was trying to look out for herself.

People have different circumstances, and as officers, we have to be more sensitive. We're supposed to be serving the public, so let's serve the public by considering their perspective and what they need. We don't serve by commanding people without cause and humiliating them. Service comes from finding out what the community wants from us and then trying to accommodate. We obviously can't accommodate every request, but we can take requests under consideration instead of defaulting to domination.

Everyone wants a warning instead of a ticket, but some people deserve a ticket because their behavior endangers others. We can still have those conversations in a respectful way. We can treat everyone with dignity and listen. It's not that hard to do. We have to start prioritizing community outreach.

How? To start, we can have community meetings and ensure the chief and other leaders in charge of making decisions actually show up. At the Criminal Justice Training Commission, the deputy director and I have made a point to sit down with the president and the vice president of each class and ask them how their time is going. We've learned so much just by asking. We just learned we were charging recruits to do their laundry. We never would have found that out without listening because we have no reason to go in the dorms. We also learned the Wi-Fi wasn't working consistently.

We're trying to have as much communication as we can in order to make positive changes and model respectful treatment, because we want them to listen and treat others with respect, too.

Every problem requires communication and working with our community leaders. I love working with the community leaders and getting to know who has their finger on the pulse of what's happening in the streets. There are experts on the ground who know where their challenges lie. They can tell me better than I can guess.

Every geographical area has its own set of strengths and weaknesses, so it's important for leaders to communicate and find out what their particular issues are and how they can solve them while doing the least amount of harm possible.

This may seem radical compared to how things are now, but it doesn't have to be. We can be that change. For example, a couple of years ago, a law passed that stated the WSCJTC had to create training on the history of race in policing, including the Latin American community and policing. We also provided training regarding the Holocaust and the Jewish communities and how we interact with them.

Why take that extra step? The more knowledge officers have, the better job they can do serving diverse communities.

If you don't know whom you're serving, you can't serve them well. At restaurants, servers don't dictate to customers what they'll eat. They introduce themselves, solicit questions, and find out what people want. The analogy isn't absolute, but if we keep in mind serving people and modeling service to recruits, we'll have better outcomes. We can still hold people accountable, but we also have a responsibility to instill a service mindset, which includes ensuring we meet recruits where they are and ensure the academy teaches students in the way they can learn.

That's where I come in.

RISING ABOVE

I've had so many experiences in my career of white men with power in the organization, even ones who were smart and fair and cared about my career, expressing confusion about what they should do differently. Even when I've confronted them about my experience, they've wondered aloud what the solution could possibly be. They are cases not of refusing to do the right thing but rather of not even knowing what the right thing was, which is still alarming to me today. That dynamic shows the importance of having a diverse workforce.

If there had been competent people of color and women in the upper echelon of leadership, they could have pointed out and helped rectify the systemic problems and ignorance. Without that diversity, though, no one was even asking the question. Instead, they picked everyone to be, look, and act like themselves.

My purpose in writing this book is to share the lessons that people who are in leadership or aspiring to leadership might not even know they need to know. It's okay if you don't know, but it's not okay if you pretend you know or don't give a shit. It's better to admit your ignorance and then seek out answers from a better source. That willingness to be vulnerable helps you learn. Vulnerability is disarming and gets relationships to the point where you can find a common understanding and move forward.

When you're hiring people, stop looking for people just like yourself. So many people are poor judges of character. They don't know how to behave, and they only seek to be comfortable. They find hires who make them feel comfortable instead of the most qualified people for the job. That approach does not strengthen teams and organizations. Thinking you're already good enough does not lead to self-examination or growth.

CHALLENGES CAN BE THE FUEL FOR CHANGE

Do you remember the letter I mentioned in Chapter 2? The one that was posted on the public union forum after I placed first on the sergeant exam? The one that essentially said I was incapable of the job and that the system was rigged to have put me in it in the first place? The one that argued there was no possible way I could have scored as high as I did on the test?

Well, I reread that letter in the process of writing this book. And even after all this time, it still hurt me. I'm strong, but I'm human.

People like the ones who supported or at least turned a blind eye to the egregious bullying that letter represents are in the force to this day. They might no longer be talking about me, but they still argued that too many African American troopers scored too high on the promotion tests, so we must have cheated. These racist officers have decided they're playing by the rules, while people like me couldn't possibly advance except through nefarious means. The assumption is we don't inherently have the skills.

At the same time, so many people think somehow racism, sexism, and other prejudices are "fixed" and don't exist anymore. Just recently, though, we had a case in which someone made a harassing comment. He doesn't see the problem with his conduct and wants to be reinstated. His agency hired a lawyer on his behalf. Too many people think the world used to be close-minded but is equal now. In fact, the old behaviors persist.

Some people can't even hear that the letter maligning me came from a place of racism and sexism. They think it was one individual criticizing another individual with equal standing based on the specifics of the situation. That's simply not true. On the same promotion list I was criticized as being too "junior" to be on, there was a white male with less tenure. Nobody said one damn word about him taking the test, and they certainly didn't write a letter.

If you've seen discrimination like this up close, it's impossible to ignore. If I go home and tell one of my African American friends about the letter, they'll immediately say, "Girl, I know." They get it because they live it every day. African American people navigating white systems know what I'm talking about, but we're also largely left to endure the treatment on our own.

I'm fortunate to have people of many different races in my life, and many of them have lived through the experiences with me. They know what it means to keep running into barriers despite being smart and results-driven. The discrimination can be subtle, too. I do have a job—I haven't been completely shut out of employment. I can't imagine how frustrating it would feel to be highly qualified and not find a position anywhere.

I'm also fortunate to have reached a point in my career where I feel secure. I have my retirement, and no one can take that away from me. As I pursue new endeavors, I have a sense of not having to take any shit, which is very different from when I first started out. I'm grateful to have made it here.

In my life, I've found ways to take the terrible things that happen to me, like the letter, and use them as fuel to stoke change. Instead of silencing me, that experience inspired me to make sure others know what it can be like for an African American woman officer in an agency dominated by white men, with the intent that some of them will engage in changing the culture for the better. All the rude, nasty behavior becomes fodder for me to explain what happens and what needs to improve. Those challenges offer me opportunities.

Over the years, people in the patrol would ask me if I was going to write a book one day. I'd always laugh and say, "Yes, I am. You just wait for it." This book is another example of my following through and completing what I say I will. I'm taking care of my own dream while also trying to help the world of law enforcement evolve.

I don't want to beat anyone up, but I do want to hold up a mirror. If they see how they kicked my ass, I hope they'll turn around and kick their own ass.

8

What's Next? Notes on Legacy and Reform

On January 12, 2022, Spencer graduated from the very training academy at which I am the executive director.

The whole time he was in training, he said he didn't want anyone to know I was his mother because he didn't want anyone to feel like he received special treatment—which he didn't. It wasn't too hard to keep that fact quiet because we have different last names, but he did let a few close friends he made during training in on our secret.

On graduation day, he honored me by having me pin his badge. Those in the crowd who didn't know I was his mother audibly gasped, and we couldn't stop smiling. It was such a moving moment. We are a team, and we always will be.

I didn't cry during the graduation ceremony, but I did the following Monday when I was at the academy and he wasn't. It hit me hard then: I wouldn't see him every day at flag ceremony. I wouldn't hear him laughing as he passed my window. It was all those little moments I'd miss, but it was also a bigger realization: we had entered a new phase of his adulting.

Spencer knows my philosophy on community, and he acknowledges that he has a lot to learn. As an officer, I pray for his safety and his ability to protect himself, but I also pray he is open to the community we serve and gives them a chance.

Sometimes, I think back to that moment when I was standing in front of his kindergarten class, all those years ago, when he'd said, "That's my mom." Fast forward, and there I was . . . standing in front of him again, only this time I was pinning his badge at graduation, watching him fulfill a lifelong dream.

Pride swells in my heart when I think of how far we've come.

That's my son.

* * *

Our state is working on a number of reform laws right now. The other day, I spoke to a reporter who commented he hadn't ever seen so many reform laws passed at once. However, I reflect back on the Civil Rights Movement, how much work had to happen, and how many laws had to pass for us to reach the point where we are right now. Abolishing segregation was an enormous effort. Having kids peacefully go to school together and drink from the same water fountain didn't happen overnight.

This won't either.

That said, I'm a believer in process and following the steps. I'm proud that today, I play a part in making those steps.

At the end of the day, law enforcement officers have the upper hand in a given situation. That is just a fact. They need to stay within the boundaries of good conduct as well as writing up everything that happens afterward so that justice can truly be served.

Every interaction is an opportunity to help someone and model ethical behavior, period. My role in shaping how that looks moving forward is a huge part of my legacy, and it's one I'm proud to share with you in this chapter.

COMMUNITY POLICING

The current reforms are terrifying to police in many ways because a large number of them think the laws indicate public hate toward them. They want communities to like them and see them as good people. They see themselves as working for the people and risking their lives every day. As true as those facts may be, do these officers present themselves as part of the community and make their role clear? In smaller communities, it's easier to be part of the community. If you only have fifteen officers, chances are you know the high school principal, the pastor of the largest church, and so on.

Those community policing dynamics don't always come easily in larger districts, though. If you have 1,100 commissioned troopers, five assistant chiefs, and various other layers of management, you have to be intentional about creating community. I don't actually see it as that hard, because in general, people don't want to be at odds with the police. That conflict has arisen from a history of events, but most citizens don't want the negative relationship to continue, so it doesn't have to persist. At the same time, people don't want the police to push them around or disrespect them.

We've trained police officers to take control and use force. We talk about "ask, tell, make"—in other words, an officer will ask someone, command someone, and then force them to follow an order. In police training, this is referred to as "command presence." The community, though, feels disrespected. If you ask someone to step out of the car, they ask why, and then you drag them out of the car, it's not a good relationship. The person in the car feels they have a right to ask a question. Taking orders without a reason is scary. Police might see questions as stalling so the suspect can hurt them, whereas the community often simply wants to protect themselves and understand what's going on.

ACCOUNTABILITY

Another recent reform law says that at decertification hearings, the officer in question has to facilitate a review of their social media accounts (if their social media is related to their possible decertification). The police officers went crazy when this bill passed, yet no one testified against that part of it during the legislative hearings. After the fact, they turned it into the WSCJTC "snooping on everyone's social media," which isn't what the law says. Plus—let's be honest—nobody has time to (or wants to) do that. When the bill was up for consideration, no one testified against that part of it. So why is everyone angry?

It's gotten to the point where I don't want to listen to my voicemail, because people call me names and have all kinds of out-ofproportion reactions. I called one man back, and he appreciated my taking the time. I explained the law has been taken out of context, that it is a law and not my personal whim, and what its purpose is. Once we had that conversation, he thought it made more sense. The WSCJTC isn't trying to conduct surveillance on everyone's social media; that review only comes into play in particular situations where there are already issues with the officer's conduct, and their social media activity is implicated in some way.

When we have probable cause to believe a civilian is engaged in criminal activity, we might search their trunk or their cellphone. Officers understand that dynamic, but they don't want to be policed themselves. Searching their social media with cause is no different, though. The police need to be accountable, too. Instead of resisting and stalling at every turn, officers need to step up and demonstrate behavior that encourages trust and confidence.

MAKING BETTER DECISIONS

We have to change the way we do business, and change upsets people. But the reforms don't have to be as scary as officers think they are. They make the community safer for everyone. They emphasize de-escalation and slowing down the process. My trainers have arrived at the formula that if you have distance and shielding, you have time to make a good decision. I'm not talking about an active shooter situation, but in a contentious traffic stop, for instance, you don't have to escalate physically.

Could you give instructions over the PA and make allowances for someone blowing off steam versus posing a threat? Could you give them time to calm down before finding out what's going on or taking them into custody? If there's a life or death situation, we have the tools to prevail. If you need to cover the distance and intervene, you will. However, we don't need to resort to those tactics when they aren't warranted—in fact, we shouldn't. Keeping a safe distance and listening prevents the need to engage with force.

The police do have some reasonable complaints regarding the implementation timeline of reforms. Legislators wanted to calm down the community, so they were extremely aggressive with the timelines, which doesn't allow the rollout to be as orderly as it should be. The WSCJTC has a very small staff to respond to everything coming down the pike. Also, in their haste, legislators gave us some contradictory directives. For example, they said we shouldn't use anything over fifty caliber but should use less-lethal alternatives, e.g., beanbags; however, the launcher for the beanbags is over fifty caliber. Had we had more time, we would have realized and could have had the chance to share that information, but everything moved very fast, even though much of the content is great.

CLOSETED VIEWS STILL COUNT

In some ways, the reforms don't go as far as people think they should. Officers are up in arms about the social media issue, but you can still be a racist cop and make racist social media posts without losing your certification. That situation scares me. How can you be fair to people if you already hate them? The largest percentage of African American people in Washington live in Pierce and King counties, so I don't trust an openly racist cop to make safe, unbiased decisions while working in those areas—especially when it comes to arresting an African American or a person of color.

One officer was making racist posts, but his sheriff couldn't fire him. He could be punished but not decertified. If someone openly exhibits racism during the academy, we could let them go, but it's hard. White leaders sometimes fall back on asking whether people should be fired simply for holding particular views, but they need to start thinking outside their own lane. "Views" don't seem threatening to a fellow white man who isn't in danger, but they can mean life or death to a person of color interacting with that openly racist officer. It impacts the community the officer is supposed to serve.

If you're white and your server at a restaurant hates white people, wouldn't you be worried about what they might do to your food? The same issue comes into play with officers, prosecutors, and judges.

If they have a bias against people of color, then people of color have reason to fear they won't receive justice because they're up against stereotypes about criminality. Think about how many men the Innocence Project has finally helped release from prison because they were wrongly convicted of rape when it turns out the DNA didn't match. If you take forty years of someone's life, they can't get that time back, no matter how much money you give them.

Yes, some people have committed the crime, but in order to administer justice, the representatives of the law need to treat everyone with impartiality.

CONTINUAL IMPROVEMENT

Some officers resisting reform say that revamped laws and regulations impede their ability to do their job, but that's simply not the case. Those laws and regulations are about setting tighter parameters for the sake of protecting everyone's rights, not just officer's or white people's rights. These changes also inherently ask us to open our hearts and minds to taking a different approach and learning how to do better. We need to know when we're not doing as well as we could and improve.

What do Microsoft, Tesla, and Amazon do every day? Like it or not, they focus on doing the work better. Look at how many iterations there have been of computers, cellphones, and other kinds of technology. Those came to exist because people sit around constantly trying to figure out how to improve their products and meet people's needs. They constantly push out updates and upgrades. In medicine, doctors can now do laparoscopic surgery and use robots, whereas in the past, they'd remove essential body parts.

I'm not sure why police would think we're exempt and somehow the only profession that doesn't need to get better, both for ourselves and our communities. Yes, I want law enforcement to be safe. I don't ever want to lose an officer. It is awful. But I don't want to lose a community member either. To kill a kid with a fake gun who is just playing in a park? His actions should not turn deadly because we don't know how to communicate. Why kill a person in thirty seconds when you could engage the shielding and distance that creates the time to make a better decision?

The laws around certification in the state of Washington are trying to prevent people who should not be cops from being cops. The laws also aim to stop cops from transferring somewhere else when they come under fire in their current agency. If you're not doing well in any agency, you shouldn't be able to go to another agency and cause havoc there. Legislators worked to block that loophole. Recently, in another state, an officer was terminated for excessive use of force, but then he was appointed interim chief at another agency. This action impacts the credibility of the profession.

WHAT DO WE DO ABOUT THE BAD APPLES?

The Seattle Police Department is one of the few agencies in the state that tried to see whether their officers attended the January 6 insurrection. They terminated a couple for lying and disciplined a couple others. Of course, Seattle is not the only agency whose officers were at the insurrection. Following through with consequences is important because that day was not a peaceful demonstration, no matter what some try to say. An officer lost his life, others committed suicide, and others were seriously injured or threatened with racial epithets. It boggles my mind that officers can be so hellbent on doing whatever they want that they're even willing to be a part of a group that would harm other officers. Rooting out racism and biases—in other words, the "bad apples"—is as tough as you think it might be. Actually, it's tougher.

In thinking about how to deal with "bad apples," I hope we can create a culture that supports *good* apples in calling out bad behavior in others as well as not being ashamed to admit their own biases and work to fix them. Police tell me all the time they'd be the first one to turn in someone who shouldn't be certified, but I always ask, "Will you?" Because officers do protect bad cops. It depends on the offense, of course, and I think some officers turn a blind eye to racism because they see some of those biases in themselves and don't know what to do.

LEGACY

You know by now that my son started the academy this year. My husband taught him how to shine his boots.

"If someone tells you to get in the dirt, you'd better refuse," I joked with him. "Because your boots are so clean."

"If someone tells me to get in the dirt, I'll get in the dirt," he replied. "Because that's what you taught me."

I also asked him why he ran around looking for boot polish when he knew we had some, and he said it was because I'd taught him to come prepared, not to expect someone else to have what he needed. Those moments feel gratifying to me, because I want him to be stronger through the example I've set. I want him to know what's right, how to do the right thing even when it's hard, and how to find his drive when he wants to give up.

It's okay to decide something isn't for you anymore, but not to give up. People sometimes confuse the two, but they're not the same. I want the next generation of women and minorities to know the community needs them. Why? Because WE ARE the community. The community is made up of all of us. Even when people try to make you feel like you don't belong, you are supposed to be there. You are going to help others by getting to the finish line with dignity.

We must help each other be strong through the difficult times as our society still works to integrate and incorporate women and minorities in predominantly white male fields. I was a hairdresser/flight attendant/communications major. Besides Vernestine and Felicia, I had guidance from people who passed through my life. If I could do it, I have no doubt anyone else who wants it and puts their heart into it can, too. People like to cast a mystique around law enforcement and act like only Superman or Wonder Woman could do it, but we're just regular people.

MOTIVATION

When things get tough, I've always remembered my son is watching me. What I did mattered so much to him and still does. As I encountered negative people and experiences in the academy and thought of giving up, I knew Spencer was counting on me. From the very first time he took me for kindergarten show and tell and said, "That's my mom," I knew he looked up to me. I was in uniform and thought it would be so much fun, but I had tears streaming down my face because his admiration meant so much. I'll never forget that moment. I hadn't been out of the academy for more than four months.

When I do speaking engagements, young girls have always come up and talked to me. They want to know how I achieved what I have, and grown women have had the same attitude. I've realized how much my presence and perseverance mean to them, so I couldn't just quit. I was creating a path for other people. Until it's done, it can't be done.

I wasn't the first woman, but I connected with people. Even my first sergeant told me people never connected with her in the same way when she was in uniform. I built bridges by connecting with people.

I want people to know *this is your police force* and *these are your state troopers*. You have a right and an opportunity to pursue this career if you feel called to. It's not a job for superheroes; it's a job for people. I'm internally tough and have fortitude, but I never try to put on tough airs because I want the people I serve to know I'm a real person.

Even if you don't have a child to motivate you, you have a community that counts on you. Never lose sight of what your community expects of you, and feel proud. Everyone has someone looking up to them. My friends looked up to me, too. Vernestine was proud of me just for making decisions about my life.

Conclusion

Is policing a racist institution?

The million-dollar question—and one you might have for me. I understand why. I'll do my best to answer it.

There *is* racism within the police profession, but I do not think most police officers are racist. A great deal of bias gets built in through training and recruitment, which tends to be mostly white men recruited and taught by white men who did not grow up in the inner city or have exposure to diverse communities. The world is still largely segregated, which I can attest to, as my husband and I are the only African American couple in our neighborhood. There are some white people married to African American people, but we're the only African American couple.

If you live in a largely segregated area, then think about your exposure to people of other races. When I see my white neighbors having guests over, I don't see African American people going into their homes. That lack of interaction with people different from them would affect their ability to serve the community without bias.

For example, a WSP trooper flew a confederate flag over his patrol car at his house, which sent a very intentional message. Plenty of white officers saw it as a "freedom of speech" issue or individual's business instead of something dangerous to the community.

What officers do on their "own time," though, does impact the community. An officer who smokes marijuana in off-hours will get fired, for instance. Our job has regulations and requirements, and those should extend to racist actions like linking a confederate flag to the police. The department tried to say they'd investigated and found the flag was a family heirloom, but I saw it, and it looked new.

Through that experience, I learned how many white men I worked with seemed caring but did not actually have empathy or understanding for others. They didn't mean intentional harm, but as bystanders who weren't open to listening or understanding why the flag could be a big deal, they showed they weren't open to learning. One of them called my husband after George Floyd was murdered. By calling his "African American friend," he wanted to feel like he was doing something good.

I'm not here to make people feel good, though; I'm here to make a difference. When people dig in on their mistakes, I'm coming for them. Real change is hard and requires more than a phone call to make yourself feel better. It might, for instance, require you to expose yourself to people who don't live like you not because you *have* to, but because you *want* to. Because creating opportunities to connect with others is important. There are different layers of privilege you can't understand in a monolithic area, even if you grew up in poverty or with other hardships.

I see people who have those blinders on not as inherently racist but certainly as having biases they're choosing not to deal with. That refusal to listen, learn, and grow prevents us from making positive reforms as quickly as we could. We all have some sort of bias, but we can choose to address it and grow, or we can double down and refuse, which has negative consequences. We don't always have to agree, but if we want to move forward, we have to listen. In order to grow, we have to be willing to be comfortable in an uncomfortable space.

LAW ENFORCEMENT LEADER? THIS MESSAGE IS FOR YOU

First, thank you for reading this far. That is a phenomenal first step. But let's call it like it is: reading isn't the same as doing. What I'm going to ask you now is to listen. That's a verb for a reason. You have to actively do it.

First, stop selecting only people who look like you. Appreciate the differences people from other backgrounds bring to your organization. When you recruit women and minorities, make them feel welcome. Diversity might seem cut and dry on paper, but true inclusion takes more work.

The other night, I talked to an officer who told me how the African American officers don't feel like a part of the group and included in the guild. They feel left out of the fold. I've seen this story play out again and again. My deputy director and I talked about how he tried to become a trooper. He was about to graduate from the University of Washington, but the patrol turned him down three times. He's driven and determined, so it almost brings me to tears when he tells me he sees the pictures of my husband and me in our uniforms and wonders why they wouldn't accept him.

As a new trooper, not only did I not feel included, I also constantly heard reminders that I was the only black woman in the agency. Like I was going to forget it?

People continually asked me whether I knew and was okay with being the only one. I'd been an African American woman for thirty-five years at that point, so yeah, I was okay with myself. But clearly they didn't know what to do with me.

Break the cycle.

Looking back on it, I realize I was trying to make *them* feel comfortable instead of them trying to make me feel comfortable, because I wanted the job so badly. I wanted them to know that I could adjust. I wanted to show them I could pivot and work through anything— and I did, but I have scars from the experience.

I told them as a flight attendant I didn't get to pick who the passengers were or the destination of the flight. I could go for days and never see another person who looked like me, and I managed. They felt impressed with my answer. You could see them relax because I wasn't making a big deal about the situation. But that doesn't give you an out.

If nobody is in the pipeline to promote, ask yourself why and what you've done to perpetuate a diversity-less pipeline. Before pointing at African American people or women for "not applying" or "not being qualified enough," notice the other four fingers pointing back at you.

If you have no diversity in your organization, blame yourself. If you accept the praise when your organization does well, then take responsibility for the deficits, too. You set the tone and the culture as a leader.

If you've read this, I already know you care and want to do better. Let's do it together.

COMMUNITY? THIS MESSAGE IS FOR YOU

If you're not directly involved in law enforcement, there's still plenty to learn and think about regarding policing, community relations, the potential for reform, and how you might fit in with the solution. Your experiences with the police are yours, and I don't question those. I will say, in Washington we have 11,000 commissioned officers and 3,000 corrections officers who work in the jails. We're in the middle of a shift and a change, so it's important to figure out a way for community and law enforcement to communicate with one another.

The police are supposed to be serving your community. If they're not engaging appropriately, then it's your responsibility to reach to the top and alert your chief, sheriff, council member, or the mayor. You can talk to the city manager. If you're not getting what you need, then make sure you're a part of the selection process for the next chief. The process is transparent and community-based, but most people don't get involved until the city has already picked someone. Also don't just look at people at face value. Consider the experience they bring. They don't have to be an African American person, a person of color, or a woman, but they do have to know how to interface with all different kinds of people, because it's only fair.

As a community member, you are empowered to participate. Police are supposed to help you, so it's not rocking the boat to hold them accountable. I will say the current dynamic feels like the community is on the attack and the police are on the retreat, which isn't a sustainable way of doing business. I think we should lodge our concerns and complaints properly. Police are not a monolith, just like communities are not a monolith.

CHANGES AHEAD

There's a way to hold everyone accountable if we're willing to engage. I welcome the challenges that are being put forward right now with law enforcement. I welcome the change, growth, and development we'll see as a result. I'm not afraid of people quitting. I wish them luck. If they're so afraid of being held accountable that they want to leave, then that's probably the right decision. If they want to be a public handler rather than a public servant, then they should go.

The community should have a say in how we police them. If we say they don't understand, we're missing the point. They understand how they feel, and we have to work to understand those feelings.

I want us to be more open to the community we're serving and to learn as much as we can about them. Read books, educate yourself, and cultivate critical thinking. Adapt how you implement procedures to the situation at hand. We all want to be heard, including the people we serve. Imagine if the citizen you're interacting with were your family member or your dear friend instead of just a suspect. How would you treat them differently?

We can build bridges to connect with our communities. Some people don't want to stay in the profession because it's changing, but wanting to maintain the status quo implies you think we're already perfect. We're clearly not. If crime is going up, is it because we aren't mean and militaristic enough—or is crime going up because we've lost the connection to our community? I think it's the latter, so how do we get that connection back?

Of course you're not going to connect with everyone, because there are people out there who truly mean harm—such as rapists and murderers—but they're a very small population. Let's find a way to protect the vast majority, who are good, from those few bad actors. Our job is to make regular, decent community members feel safe, which requires listening to and working together with them.

If someone shoplifts because they're starving, they aren't a hardened criminal. How can we provide better services for people who don't have money? One size does not fit all when it comes to police response. People who have mental challenges need support rather than criminalization. We can show compassion instead of jumping to conclusions and using force.

My approach to my life's work is a combination of strength and compassion. I've earned authority, so I have a responsibility to use it wisely and with compassion. It's hard to be an officer—missing holidays with your family, facing confrontation on the job, grappling with emotionally-charged situations daily. It takes internal strength to power through. Sometimes you have to be physically strong just to keep your body in shape and keep moving. You also have to be smart enough to overpower challenges, not only physically but also mentally and emotionally. You also have to be compassionate, though. People don't have to look, act, or be like you to earn that compassion. Many of them have endured much worse than you or I have. Some people do not have a clear path forward. Purely through their being human, they deserve your care.

Even with all my challenges, I consider myself fortunate because I did have a path forward even in my darkest hours, so I want to extend grace to others who might not be as fortunate.

ASK FOR HELP

I imagine I'll be active in the law enforcement community for another three to four years in this role. I'm a quick pivoter. I have some goals around the curriculum redesign and creating an environment that helps people to feel welcomed and empowered.

I address all the classes of new recruits, and I tell them the same thing I told my son: if they experience struggles with academics or any aspect of the journey, stop one of us in the hall. Let us help you be successful.

This lesson applies outside the walls of my building. Don't suffer in silence. People want to be a resource to you. By asking for help, you pave the way for the next generation.

I have similar advice for the community as for the new recruits: let us help you. Tell us what you need. If something isn't working, seek out the resources to make it better. We are here to serve.

If you're a leader, don't make yourself so unapproachable that people won't come to you for help. Invite people to approach you and ask you for help. If those around you don't feel like they can rely on you for support, you'll be surrounded by people suffering in silence. This approach is top-down for a reason. If we treat officers that way, they will treat their public that way. In turn, we change the culture.

FUND THE POLICE

There's emphasis on defunding the police of late, but I encourage people to think about how we can *refund* the police, with compassion as a currency. Cutting police salaries will not improve policing. Take money from the cops if you want to, but it will make hiring well-educated people more difficult. You'll lose people who need the salary and benefits. If someone can make the same money at Home Depot, why would they risk their life?

Yes, there are conversations we can have around changing priorities rather than "defunding." We can add social workers and mental health support rather than penalizing law enforcement. We can redistribute and reinvest to prevent problems, recognizing police have a role in improving their implementation.

We have to start somewhere. We all do.

I'm no exception. I know where *I* started, and I'm honored to have accomplished what I did in my career. When Spencer was a little boy, we would drive to the Port of Tacoma and watch the ships as they were loaded for their journey. The other day, I decided to stop on my way home from work and watch the process. I saw three little tugboats link up to drag a giant, loaded-down barge. How heavy it must have been, and how small they looked in comparison. At first glance, it looked like their job was impossible. But together, it wasn't. It reminded me of what can be done.

So let's do it. Together.

About the Author

*Spencer and I at my trooper
graduation, May 1998*

*Spencer and I at his police academy
graduation, January 2022*

Monica is the first African American female to be promoted to
the rank of sergeant, lieutenant, and captain in the history of the
Washington State Patrol (WSP).

She began her career with the WSP in 1996 as a trooper cadet. On May 1, 1998, she was commissioned as a WSP trooper and assigned to the South Seattle freeway. In addition to her duties as a trooper, Monica was the traffic reporter for KOMO-TV (ABC Affiliate Seattle) for six years. In May of 2003, out of 210 candidates, Monica placed number one on the sergeant exam and was then promoted in August of that year. She worked the following assignments: South Seattle Freeway, Office of Government and Media Relations, Homeland Security, and Office of Professional Standards. On July 16, 2013, she was promoted to lieutenant and was assigned to the Field Operations Bureau headquarters.

Monica was promoted on April 28, 2015, to captain of the Office of Government and Media Relations as the legislative liaison, where she served until June 30, 2019. On July 1, 2019, Monica was assigned as the Human Resources Division commander until she retired on August 16, 2019.

As captain and legislative liaison, some of her many accomplishments include wage increase legislation for the Washington State Troopers Association and Washington State Lieutenants and Captains Association, sexual assault kit funding, sexual assault kit tracking system, toxicology lab funding, and the Missing Native American Women Research and Report.

During Monica's career, she received numerous honors and awards, including being honored as the 2020 Brava Award recipient from Washington University Club (dinner postponed until 2022 due to the pandemic), recognition from the National Black Police Association, the Educational Excellence Award from the Washington Traffic Safety Commission, and the Black Law Enforcement Association of Washington 2019 Legacy Award.

Monica attended North Texas State University and holds a bachelor's degree in political science from Evergreen State College. She is a proud member of the Alpha Kappa Alpha Sorority, Inc. In November of 2017, Governor Jay Inslee appointed her to the Evergreen State College Board of Trustees. Over the course of her career, Monica has been active on the legislative front, including participating in the Use of Deadly Force Task Force and being appointed by Governor Inslee to the Office of Independent Investigation Advisory Board.

Monica began working at the Washington State Criminal Justice Training Commission (WSCJTC) as the Advanced Training Division manager in September 2019. Monica served as deputy director from May 2020 to March 2021. From March 1, 2021, to June 30, 2021, she filled the role of interim executive director. Then, in June 2021, Monica was appointed as the executive director of the WSCJTC.

Monica lives in the Seattle area with her husband, Johnny. She enjoys spending time with Johnny and her favorite son Spencer, knitting, FOOTBALL, theater (she has seen Hamilton fifteen times in five cities and is looking forward to sixteen), reading, traveling, styling hair, friending (new word), and putting down the ladder for the next generation.

Acknowledgments

Thank you to my mother for teaching me how to have good manners, how to speak proper English, and how to be respectful to everyone.

Thank you to my Aunt Jewell and her late husband, Frank, for always cheering me on and sharing your wisdom.

Thank you to my brother and sisters—Michael, Michelle, and Gwen —for your love and support.

Thank you to my WSP family. I miss you and appreciate the training, learning, and twenty-three years I spent with you.

9 781544 531533